A Geography of Belize

of Belize

The land and its people

Published by Cubola Productions
35 Elizabeth Street
Benque Viejo del Carmen
Belize, Central America

Editorial Consultants: Sydney Campbell, Janet Gibson, Marla Holder, Robert Leslie, Byron Rempel, Frank Panton, Carmita Ruiz, Charles Wright.

Illustrations by: Manuel González Daza
Design by A to Z Graphic Studio

Special thanks to the following persons and institutions for their assistance in the development of specific sections of this publication: Lydia Wade, Valdemar Andrade / Belize Audubon Society, Sandra Paredes / Central Statistical Office, John McGill / Coastal Zone Management Project, Eldridge Castillo / Fisheries Department, Faith Smith / Geology and Petroleum Office, Norris Hall / Belize Information Centre, UNICEF, Carlos Fuller, Justin Hall / National Meteorological Service, Vivianni Teul and Brian Holland.

Front cover photograph: Jimmie C. Smith / Islands from the Sky

Photography by: Gloria Auil, Mina Bárcenas, Gemma Comas, Cubola Archives, Abril Esquivel, Norris Hall, Jimmie C. Smith, Jack Wood.

First Edition, July 1996
6th Revised Edition, July 2002

Printed and bound in Mexico

ISBN 976 8111 05 4

A Geography of Belize
The land and its people

Part One
The Earth is Our Home

PEOPLE HAVE ALWAYS GAZED in wonder at the environment around them. We look in awe at the stars sprinkled through the sky, or at the rocks right under our feet. What we have seen has shaped our beliefs and our very way of life.

Geography is the science that studies the Earth's surface and the Earth's phenomena. It also studies the transformations that occur over time caused by both natural phenomena and by people's actions. The study of geography helps us to get the knowledge necessary to satisfy our basic needs of food, clothing and shelter.

They are the things we may take for granted that keep us alive from day to day. Take a deep breath: you have just inhaled a perfect mixture of nitrogen, oxygen, and a variety of other gases. Without this exact recipe for life, the breath you have just taken would have been your last.

The Earth is constantly creating and renewing the kinds of conditions that are necessary for our survival. At the same time, natural forces are forever changing our world. Powerful forces like earthquakes, volcanoes and erosion alter the lands we live in. Humans change the landscape around them too. We can irrigate land so that we may grow more food. But we also produce large amounts of pollution that can harm our environment.

Belize is a land rich in wildlife, plants and resources. It occupies a small portion of the land on Earth. But the management of its fertile forests and bountiful sea affects the entire world. Learning about all the wonders that make our country unique will help us to manage it better. It will also enrich our enjoyment of the world around us.

Chapter 1
Our Place in the Universe

Since people first walked on the Earth, they have looked up at the sky with wonder. Why do the stars come out at night? Why did the sun rise and set?

As people studied the heavens, they began to learn about the regular movements of the stars. They found that the positions of the objects in the sky affected their day to day life.

We may never know if far-away galaxies also support life. If they do, do you think their creatures gaze up at the sky with the same wonder as us?

Today we know that the **universe** is made up of millions of stars, **cosmic gas** and dust. The force that holds everything together is called gravity. It is this force that enables us to walk on the Earth without floating into space.

In the past, most people believed that the Earth was the centre of the universe. But powerful telescopes and spaceships have changed our ideas. We now know that the Earth revolves around the sun with eight other planets. This is called a solar system. Our solar system is just a small part of a **galaxy**. A galaxy is a system of stars held together by gravity. Far, far beyond our galaxy, there are billions of other galaxies.

Explore the night sky and draw a diagram showing the position of three constellations.

There are many other objects in the universe besides stars and planets. Asteroids are tiny planets racing through space. Meteors are smaller bodies. When they collide with the Earth they are called meteorites. Comets have long tails of gas that can sometimes be seen even without telescopes.

Even after centuries of amazing discoveries, much of the universe is still a mystery to us.

Name some of the civilizations that had a good knowledge of astronomy. Find pictures or draw some of their ancient monuments.

The First Astronomers

Who were the first astronomers, the people who studied the skies? All over the world you can find ancient groups of large standing stones, called megaliths. They are a clue that astronomers long, long ago had a good understanding of movement in the sky. Ancient people arranged the stones in geometric patterns. From studying them, we know that they

In Europe, megaliths at Stonehenge in Britain date from 2800 BC. Some of these stones weigh more than 25 tons.

Egyptian pyramids were built between 2600 BC. and 2500 BC. Almost all of them were positioned carefully, facing north-south and east-west.

were arranged to mark the rising and setting of the sun and moon at specific times of the year.

Important discoveries in **astronomy** were made throughout the world. The Babylonian, Chinese, Mesopotamian, Greek, Maya and Arab cultures were incredibly varied. But they all had in common the same goal. They wanted to make sense of the universe.

Some of these civilizations, like the Maya in Central America and the Babylonians in the Middle East, made highly accurate calendars from their observations. Astronomy was very important to the daily life of ancient cultures. They used it to know when to hold rituals. They predicted yearly floods, and organized their farming around it. The stars also guided their ships across uncharted seas, and their caravans across vast deserts.

The observations made by the ancient astronomers helped later civilizations to discover even more. Until the 14th century, people believed that the sun revolved around the Earth. Then, in the 15th century an astronomer named Copernicus proposed that the Earth, as well as the other planets, revolved around the sun. This was a very revolutionary theory that made him enemies because it went against the belief that the Earth was the centre of the universe. From that time on, we have made incredible leaps in our knowledge of the universe.

This is a pyramid in the ancient Maya city of Chichen Itza in Yucatan. On the day of the summer equinox, the sun's rays make a shadow that resembles a snake's body.

The Solar System and the Planets

Our solar system is made up of the sun and nine planets. Each planet follows its own path or orbit around the sun. Every planet has satellites or moons which orbit around them. The Earth has one moon. But some planets have many moons.

So far, our solar system is the only planetary system we have discovered. However, many astronomers think solar systems of some sort are numerous. They are spread like islands throughout the universe. The nearest known galaxy of stars is the Andromeda Galaxy. It is so far away that scientists cannot use **metres** or even **kilometres** to measure the distance. Instead they use light years. One light year equals approximately 6 trillion (6,000,000,000,000) kilometres. The Andromeda Galaxy is 2 million light years away!

A planet is a solid ball moving in an orbit around a star. It does not have light of its own. The planets are held near the sun by the force of gravity and revolve around it in orbits.

Planet Jupiter seen through a telescope, a magnifying lens that makes objects far away appear closer.

The Sun

The sun is a star around which the Earth and all of our solar system orbits. It is a huge ball of glowing gases. For us, it is the most important star among billions. Its powerful force of gravity holds our entire solar system together.

Two planets in our solar system are closer to the sun than Earth is. They are so hot – at least 800 degrees F – that life cannot exist on them. The other planets are farther from the sun than the Earth is. They are too cold for life or water. The Earth is just the right distance from the sun to provide the exact amount of heat and light needed to maintain life as we know it.

Astronomers watch the births and deaths of other stars in the universe. From these observations, they believe the sun is so powerful that it will continue to burn for 6 billion more years. Without its energy, life on Earth would cease to exist.

Explain at least three reasons why the sun is important to us. Write about what would happen if the sun ceased to exist?

Mercury is the closest planet to the sun and the second smallest in the solar system. On the side facing the sun, temperatures are very high. The other side is very cold. It takes Mercury 88 days to circle the sun at a speed of more than 70,000 km per hour.

Venus is the brightest object in the night sky apart from the moon. It is called the Morning Star and the Evening Star because it was the first "star" that our ancestors saw at the beginning and end of the day. It was named after the Roman goddess of love and beauty. Venus has the hottest surface of any planet.

Mars has always fascinated humans. Its fiery orange-red colour makes it visible in the night sky. It is also known as the Red Planet. The Romans named it after Mars, their god of war. Mars has seasons, and its days are a little over 24 hours long. There is also a thin atmosphere and ice caps at the poles.

Jupiter is the largest of all the planets. The diameter of Jupiter is ten times the diameter of the Earth. Jupiter has twelve moons.

Research and discuss some of the theories about the formation of the universe.

What are the three most important elements on Earth?

The Solar System

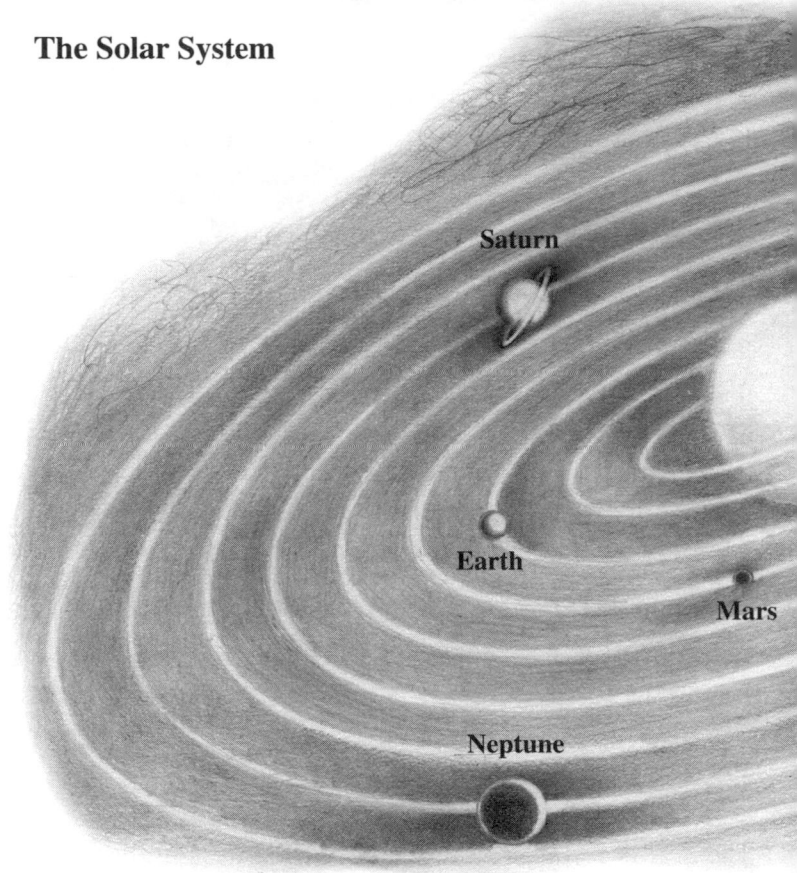

Saturn

Earth

Mars

Neptune

The Earth

Earth is the planet on which we live. We know of no other planets with life on them. Earth's orbit in our solar system is between Venus and Mars. Our planet is 150 million kilometres from the sun and travels at 29.8 km per second, or approximately 107,180 km per hour. When the Earth completes one orbit around the sun, we call it one year.

Ours is the only planet in our solar system with water. Seven-tenths of its surface is covered by the oceans. The North and South Poles are always covered with snow and ice.

Scientists have many theories about how our Earth was formed. One of them says it all started about 4.5 billion years ago. A cloud of gas and dust in space began to condense. It created a solid mass that became the planet Earth. This mass was at first very cold. Later it was melted by radioactivity.

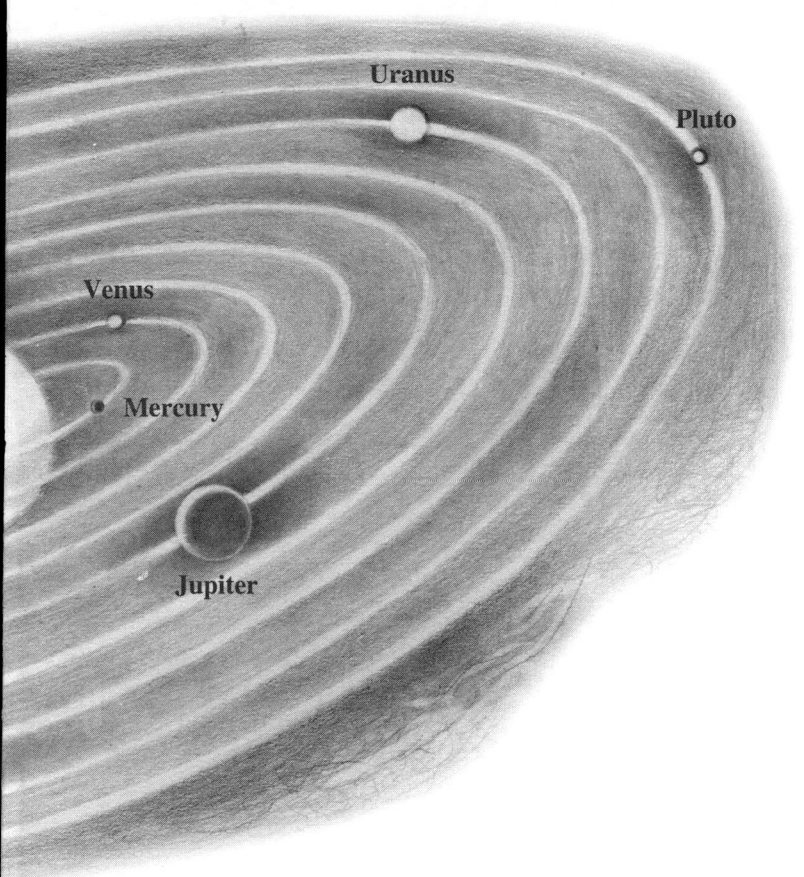

Uranus

Pluto

Venus

Mercury

Jupiter

Saturn is the most beautiful of all the planets. It is circled by a large, shinning, flat ring. About ten satellites can be seen orbiting the planet.

Uranus appears as a faint blue-green disk. Because Uranus' equator is tilted nearly 98 degrees, the planet lies on its side as it travels around the sun.

Neptune is far from the sun. It is slightly blue in appearance. Its atmosphere is probably frozen into ice particles. Neptune takes nearly 165 Earth years to complete a single orbit.

Pluto is the smallest planet in the solar system. It takes 248 years to travel once around the sun.

Heavy metals collected at the centre. Rocks floated near the surface. After millions of years, the rocks formed a hard crust. Then the atmosphere and later the oceans were formed.

The temperature of the Earth's surface is neither too hot nor too cold for life. Its gravity is enough to keep in a layer of gases. We call this the atmosphere. The atmosphere screens out dangerous rays from the sun. It also protects us from meteorites which usually burn up when they enter the atmosphere.

The Earth is not perfectly round. It is slightly flattened because it is always spinning. It rotates on its axis once every 23.9 hours. It orbits the sun once every 365 days, 6 hours, 9 minutes, and 9.54 seconds. To keep our calendar closely regulated by the sun we have to trick our calendar. So for three years each year has 365 days. The fourth year is called a leap year and has 366 days.

In groups, make a representation of the solar system and the planets' orbits around the sun. Make costumes that characterise the sun and each of the planets.

Find out about Isaac Newton's gravity laws.

The gravity of the moon is only one-sixth that of the Earth. Astronauts are only able to walk on its surface with the help of very heavy footwear.

Find out the distance from the Earth to the moon. How many days did the Apollo spacecraft take to reach the moon. At what speed did the spacecraft travel?

When does an eclipse occur? Make your own diagram of an eclipse.

The moon

The Earth has one moon that circles it once a month. The moon can be very bright at night, because it is illuminated by the sun. It circles the Earth every 27 days and 8 hours. At the same time, it completes one turn on its axis. The moon always shows the same side toward the Earth. Later we will see how the moon's orbit affects tides, the rising and falling of water in the ocean.

The moon is the nearest celestial body to Earth. It is the only one on which a spacecraft has landed.

American astronauts Neil Armstrong and Edwin Aldrin were the first men to walk on the moon. This event took place on July 20, 1969. When Neil Armstrong stepped off the ladder from his ship, he said "That's one small step for man, one giant leap for mankind." Samples brought to Earth contained no evidence of life. Rocks were similar to volcanic rocks on the Earth.

Eclipses

Through ancient times the darkening of the sky in the middle of the day caused terror among peoples who feared that the sun would disappear forever. Eclipses were often thought of as signs of bad times to come. Yet early astronomers knew that eclipses occur in regular cycles.

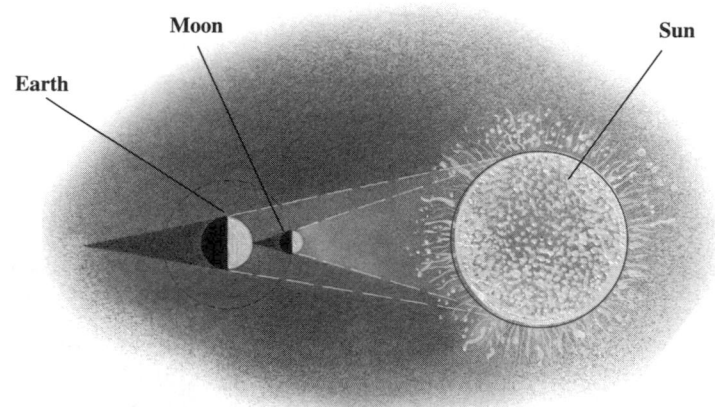

Solar eclipses are more common than lunar eclipses. There are at least two solar eclipses every year.

Daytime, Night-time, and the Seasons

The Earth makes one complete rotation on its own axis every 24 hours. This gives us daylight when our part of the Earth faces the sun.

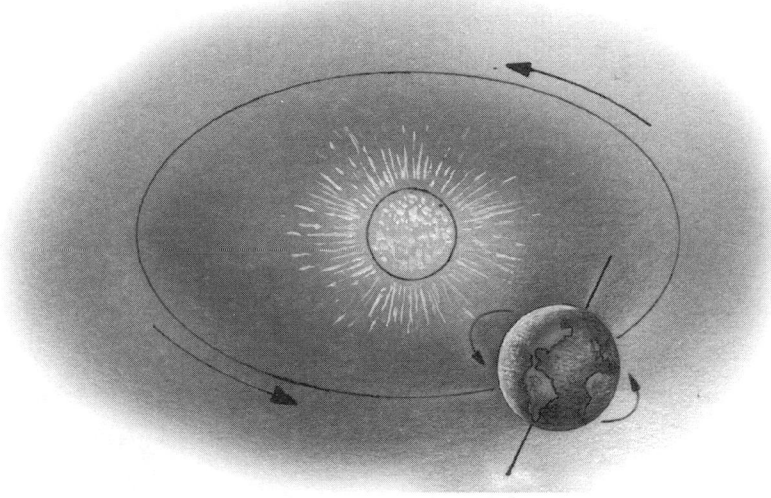

At any one point of the globe, the number of daylight hours varies throughout the year.

When our part of the Earth is turned away from the sun, we have the darkness of night. The Earth's axis may be imagined as a line that joins the North and South Poles.

Because the Earth's axis is tilted, the sun's rays strike at different angles as the Earth circles the sun.

This is why parts of the Earth have different climates. The equator is the imaginary line around the middle of the Earth. Because places near the equator are always closest to the sun, they are usually always warm.

Because the Earth is tilted, the areas north and south of the equator change in temperature more than places near the equator. Sometimes the surface of the Earth is close to the sun. At other times it is far away.

As you travel north or south from the equator, the hours of daylight and darkness change more during the year. In Belize, the amount of daylight we have changes only a little. As you go further north to the United States, the amount of daylight may change by four hours during the year. At the poles, the

Find a country on the equator. How does living on the equator affect the clothes people wear and the types of houses people live in?

What do we call the season in the Northern Hemisphere when the sun is farthest from the Earth?

13

hours of daylight and darkness are at their highest. As we move north or south, the sun's rays also become weaker.

As the Earth revolves around the sun, the sun's rays strike it at different times through the year. When the North Pole is tilted away from the sun, the sun's rays fall on the Southern Hemisphere more. In the south it is summer. In the north it is winter. When the North Pole tilts toward the sun, the north gets more of the sun's rays. Then it is summer in the north and winter in the south.

Winter in the Northern Hemisphere.

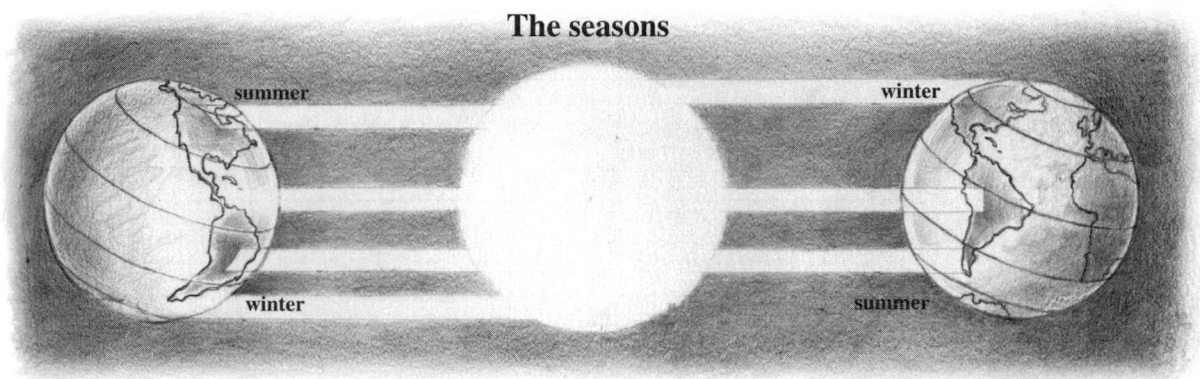

The seasons

summer

winter

winter

summer

Any day in the tropics.

🖊 *List some of the characteristics that best describe the climate of the region you live in.*

The Earth's Climates

An area's **climate** depends on its location on the Earth's surface. Latitude is important in determining climate. But wind and rain patterns, as well as altitude also have an effect on the climate. The sea influences the climate along the coast. Coastal areas have less extreme climates. This is because the sea loses heat more slowly than the land. Altitude is also important: high mountain areas might have a cold climate even in tropical regions.

To help define climate, scientists study the conditions of the atmosphere over a long period of time. They take measurements of temperature, rainfall, humidity and atmospheric pressure and wind direction.

We divide the world's climate into five major categories: equatorial, tropical, warm temperate, cool temperate and cold climate zones.

14

Geographic Coordinates

If you want to tell your friends how to get to your house, it helps to give them directions from a place you all know, such as your school or a main street. In the same way, geographers divide the world into sections so they all have the same starting point. They use imaginary lines on the globe called geographic coordinates. The geographic coordinates are latitude and longitude.

Latitude is measured in degrees and divides the globe in half horizontally. It is the distance north or south from any place on the Earth measured from the equator.

Longitude is also measured in degrees. It divides the globe in half vertically. This way we can measure distances from east to west. The prime meridian is the starting point for measuring longitude. It divides the globe into the Western and Eastern Hemispheres.

On a world map find the prime meridian and the equator. Give the geographic coordinates of Belize, Great Britain, Japan and Argentina.

List five major countries in the Northern Hemisphere and five countries in the Southern Hemisphere.

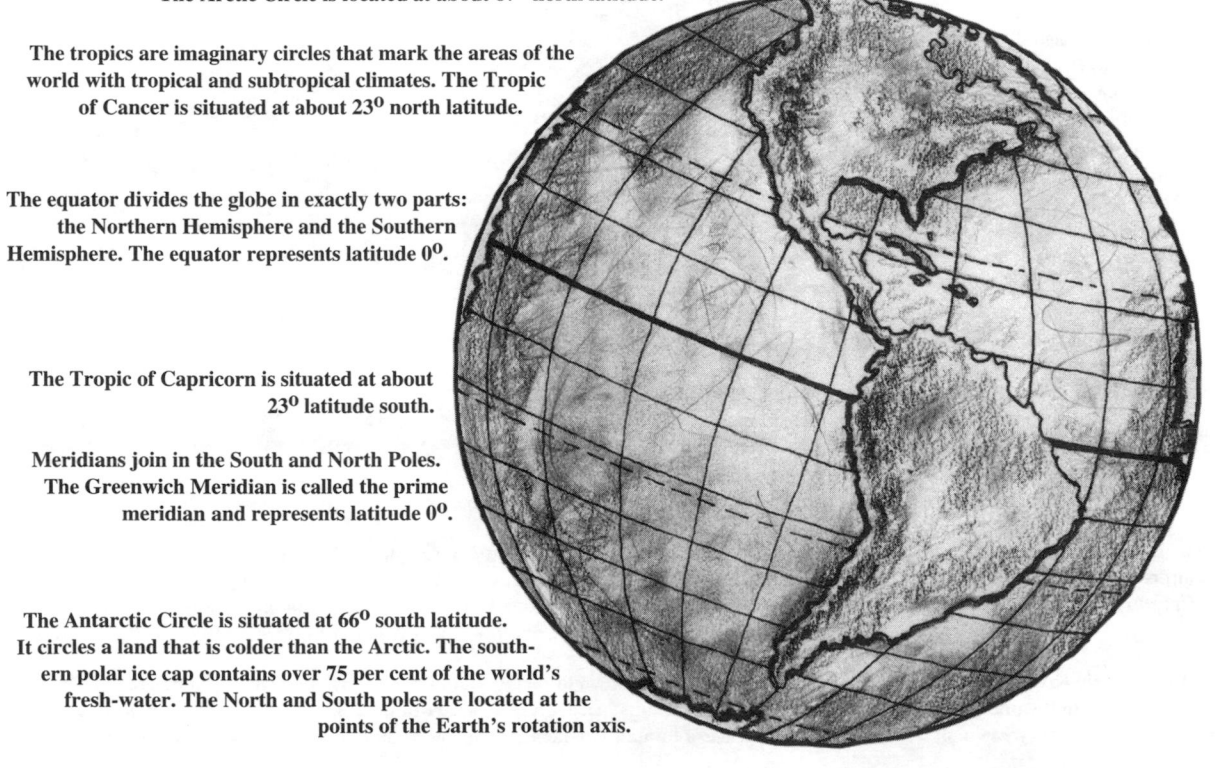

The Arctic Circle is located at about 67^0 north latitude.

The tropics are imaginary circles that mark the areas of the world with tropical and subtropical climates. The Tropic of Cancer is situated at about 23^0 north latitude.

The equator divides the globe in exactly two parts: the Northern Hemisphere and the Southern Hemisphere. The equator represents latitude 0^0.

The Tropic of Capricorn is situated at about 23^0 latitude south.

Meridians join in the South and North Poles. The Greenwich Meridian is called the prime meridian and represents latitude 0^0.

The Antarctic Circle is situated at 66^0 south latitude. It circles a land that is colder than the Arctic. The southern polar ice cap contains over 75 per cent of the world's fresh-water. The North and South poles are located at the points of the Earth's rotation axis.

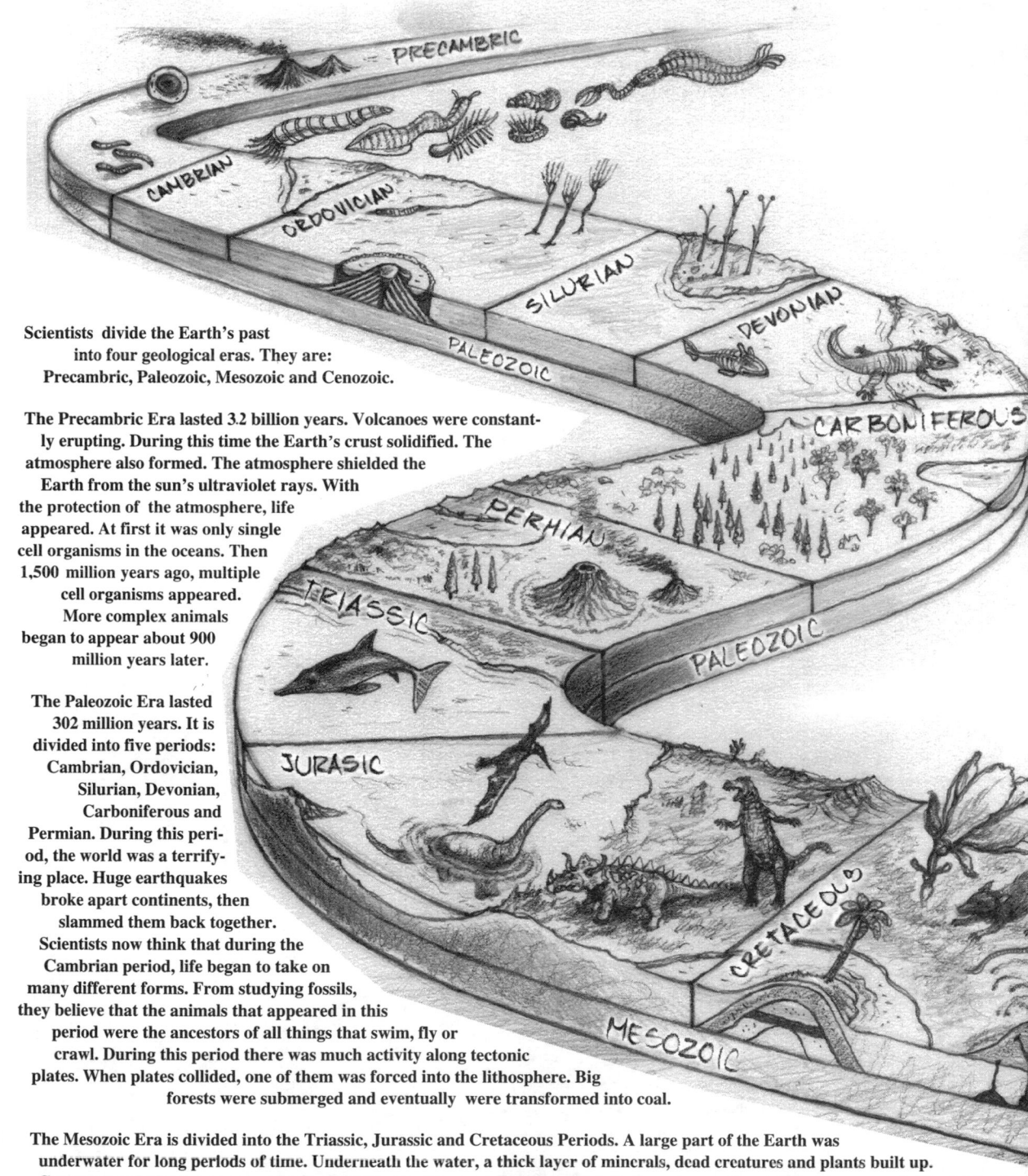

Scientists divide the Earth's past into four geological eras. They are: Precambric, Paleozoic, Mesozoic and Cenozoic.

The Precambric Era lasted 3.2 billion years. Volcanoes were constantly erupting. During this time the Earth's crust solidified. The atmosphere also formed. The atmosphere shielded the Earth from the sun's ultraviolet rays. With the protection of the atmosphere, life appeared. At first it was only single cell organisms in the oceans. Then 1,500 million years ago, multiple cell organisms appeared. More complex animals began to appear about 900 million years later.

The Paleozoic Era lasted 302 million years. It is divided into five periods: Cambrian, Ordovician, Silurian, Devonian, Carboniferous and Permian. During this period, the world was a terrifying place. Huge earthquakes broke apart continents, then slammed them back together. Scientists now think that during the Cambrian period, life began to take on many different forms. From studying fossils, they believe that the animals that appeared in this period were the ancestors of all things that swim, fly or crawl. During this period there was much activity along tectonic plates. When plates collided, one of them was forced into the lithosphere. Big forests were submerged and eventually were transformed into coal.

The Mesozoic Era is divided into the Triassic, Jurassic and Cretaceous Periods. A large part of the Earth was underwater for long periods of time. Underneath the water, a thick layer of minerals, dead creatures and plants built up. Creatures and plants grew eagerly. During this era dinosaurs first appeared. In the same era they totally disappeared. Our highest mountain chains such as the Himalayas, the Andes and the Rocky Mountains were formed during this period.

The Cenozoic Era is divided into Tertiary and Quaternary periods. Flowering plants, mammals and primates appeared. They were very similar to the ones we know today. Some animal and plant species, however, are now extinct. In this period, about two million years ago, we find the first evidence of human-like beings. The oldest human remains have been found in Africa.

Chapter 2
Our Planet Earth

Since it formed about 4,600 million years ago, the Earth has been in constant evolution. There are many theories about how it began.

Scientists believe that it took 1,000 million years before life appeared. It started as very simple forms, like bacteria and algae. More complex animals have existed only for the past 570 million years. Since then, most life forms have constantly evolved. Others, like dinosaurs, have disappeared.

The Earth's climate also has experienced many changes since it was formed. At least eight times in the life of our planet the temperatures dropped so low that large portions of the planet were covered by ice. The last of these glacial periods occurred 15,000 to 20,000 years ago

The Earth is still changing. Some changes occur because of natural causes. The movements of the Earth's crust still cause earthquakes. Volcanoes erupt and the continents are still drifting apart very slowly. Weather can change the Earth too. Hurricanes can change the coastline permanently. Rivers erode the landscape.

Through carelessness, humans also change the Earth. For example, by using certain chemicals, we can harm the ozone layer in our atmosphere. Earlier we learned how the atmosphere makes life on this planet possible. In which other ways do humans change the Earth?

Find information about dinosaurs and identify the geological period in which they appeared and the one in which they disappeared.

Discuss how the study of fossils helps determine the Earth's past.

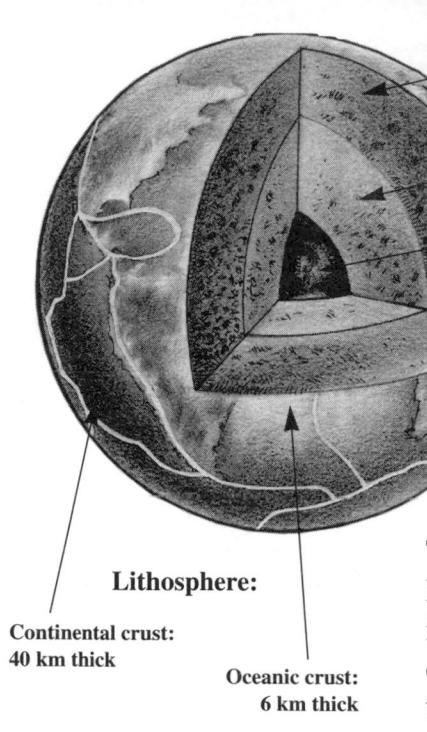

Mantle: 2,800 km thick

Central core: 2,400 km diameter

Outer core: 3,700 km

Lithosphere:

Continental crust: 40 km thick

Oceanic crust: 6 km thick

The Earth's Crust

From reading about the orbit and revolution of the Earth, you have learned that we are never standing still. At least the ground under our feet is not moving, you may think. But it is! To find out why, we have to take a journey to the centre of the Earth.

The Earth is made of several thick layers. We learned about how the Earth was formed. The heaviest minerals, nickel and iron, sank to the centre. Now they make up the solid central core of our planet. The outer core is made of nickel and iron too, but they are so hot that they are melted. The next layer is the mantle.

Above the mantle is the Earth's crust, where we live. It is hard and cracked into solid slabs called plates. These plates sit on top of the mantle. The mantle is very hot. It flows very slowly because of the molten rock beneath it. When it moves, the plates move with it. We call this movement plate tectonics.

✏ *Draw a diagram that identifies the four layers of the Earth. In which layer are the continents and oceans found.*

Tectonic Plates

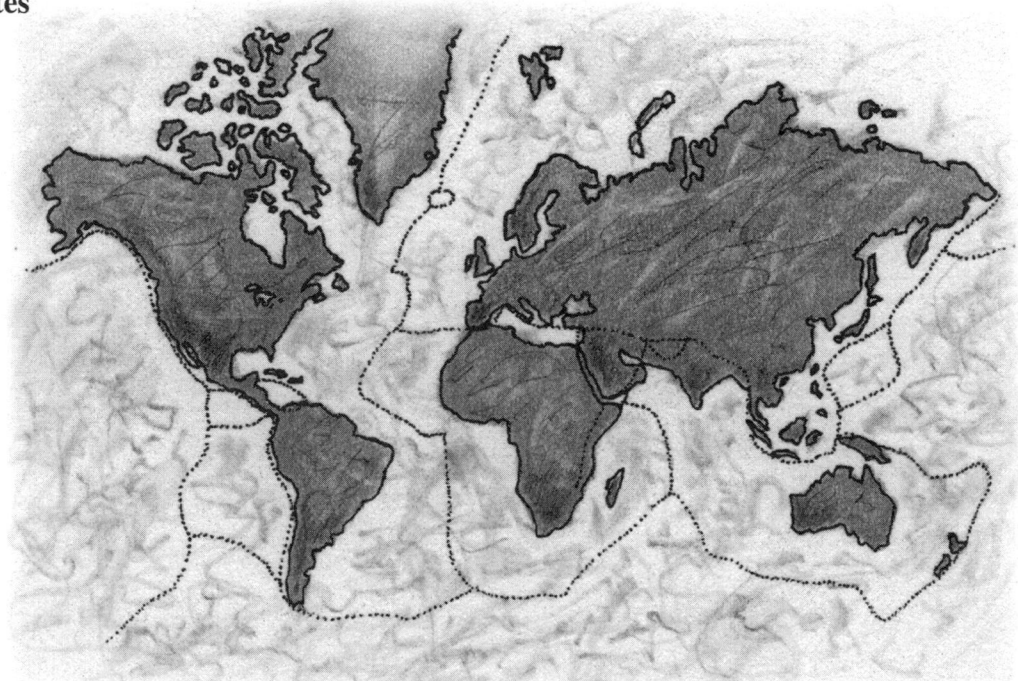

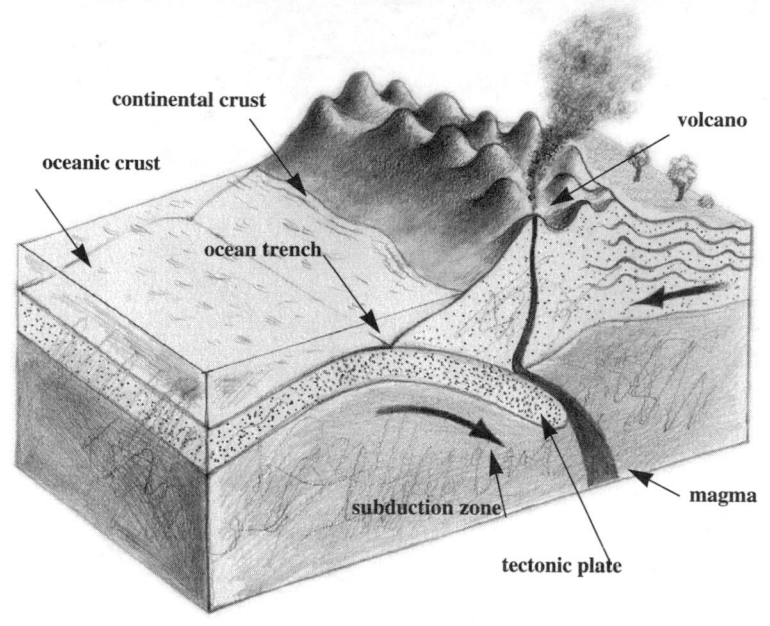

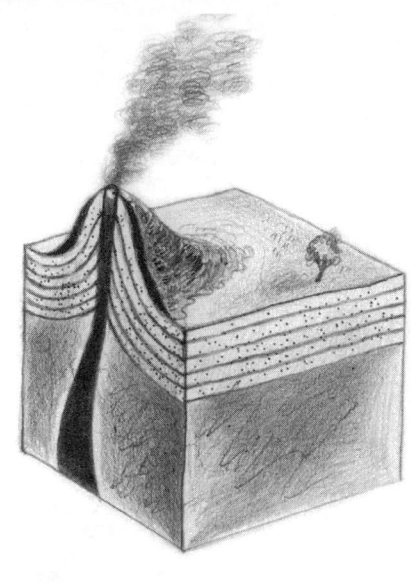

continental crust
oceanic crust
volcano
ocean trench
subduction zone
magma
tectonic plate

Mountains, Volcanoes and Earthquakes

Mountains and mountain chains are made in two ways. One is by the pressure of tectonics. The other is by the violent explosion of volcanoes.

The edges of tectonic plates are under great pressure. When two plates move towards each other the pressure is very high. What happens when you push two books together? First they move upwards in the middle. Then, eventually, one book moves below the other book. This is what happened to our crust. When plates moved together mountain chains and deep ocean trenches were formed.

Volcanoes happen when magma from the Earth's interior escapes through cracks in the crust. Sometimes volcanoes explode violently. They throw up ashes, rocks, gases and lava. Volcanoes can cause great disasters. But they can also form mountains. When the molten rock cools, new land is built up. Sometimes they form whole islands. Many islands in the Caribbean were formed by volcanoes.

Earthquakes happen because of friction along a plate's edges. The Earth's plates sometimes lock together until they cannot move easily and a lot of tension builds up. When they finally unlock, it causes a series of violent movements. Earthquake waves can travel long distances.

Earthquakes often cause terrible destruction. Human lives are lost and so is property. The centre of an earthquake is called the epicentre.

Name some of the countries which are often affected by earthquakes and volcanic eruptions. Note the position of these countries in relation to tectonic plates.

Make a list and find out the location of five of the world's active volcanoes. Find out some facts about a recent volcanic eruption.

Today

Gondwanaland became Africa, South America, Australasia, India and the Antarctic.

Laurasia split into North America and Asia.

The Continents

About 200 million years ago, during the Permian Period, all of Earth's land was joined in one super-continent. Scientists call this land Pangaea. But during the Cretaceous Period, Pangaea started to break up because of plate tectonics. At first it split into two big land masses. One was called Laurasia and the other Gondwanaland. By about 50 million years ago it had divided again. It formed the continents as we know them today.

When the continents joined and split again, many mountain chains were formed. When the plate carrying India collided with the Asian continent, for instance, the Himalayas mountain chain was formed.

Today we know that only 29 per cent of the Earth is covered by land. This includes the continents and thousands of small islands. The continents are still moving apart at a rate of 5 cms. per year. We call this movement continental drift.

There are seven continents:

North America, South America, Europe, Asia, Africa, Oceania and Antarctica. In them we find a great variety of landscapes. There are rivers, deserts, lakes, mountains and plains. Now let us take a closer look at each continent.

Pangaea

The Americas

The Americas, divided into the North and South American continents, stretch all the way from above the Arctic Circle in the north to just above the Antarctic Circle in the south. To make the whole trip you would have to travel 14,000 kilometres. They are bordered by the Atlantic Ocean on the east. On the west lies the Pacific Ocean. The planet's longest mountain chain runs along the west coasts of both continents. It starts in Alaska and ends in Tierra de Fuego. Along the way it has many different names. It is called the Rocky Mountains in the U.S. and Canada, the Sierra Madre in Mexico, and the Andes in South America. From reading earlier, you already know that this mountain chain formed because of plate tectonics.

The two continents cover a large area. This gives them a great variety of climates. The climates range from the cold northern and southern regions, to the tropical equatorial rainforest.

In the western parts of the North and South American continents, rivers tend to be short. Most of them have their source in the mountains, and drain into the Pacific Ocean. The rivers that drain into the Atlantic, however, are long and carry a lot of water. Many of them, like the Mississippi in North America and the Amazon in Brazil, are navigable. This means boats can travel their whole length.

The North American continent is made up of three large countries: Canada, the United States of America (U.S.) and Mexico.

Make a model of the world's continents and oceans, showing mountain chains and rivers. Label the continents and oceans.

Bring to class photographs of different countries. Group the photographs by continents and make a mural.

Mechanized wheat harvest.

New York City, at the mouth of the Hudson River.

The deep canyons and mesas of Colorado's Plateau.

21

Iguaçu Falls on the Iguaçu River at the border of Argentina, Brazil and Paraguay.

✎ *Name the main reason why Asia has a variety of climates.*

✎ *On a world map locate Mount Everest.*

An Islamic temple in the central Asian nation of Uzbekistan.

The island state of Singapore is one of Asia's major industrial and financial centres.

The central plains of Canada and the U.S. produce much of the world's food. Mexico City is the largest city in the world.

Central America is the thin land bridge that links North and South America. This is where Belize is located. Central America begins at the Isthmus of Tehuantepech, in Mexico, and extends down to Panama. With its temperate tropical climates, Central America enjoys tropical forests and abundant wildlife.

The South American continent contains one of the world's largest rivers, the Amazon River. In the thick tropical forests along the river, a large variety of plant and animal species are found. Some of the important countries in South America include Brazil, Argentina and Chile.

Asia

The continent of Asia is located in the Eastern Hemisphere. It is bordered by the Arctic Ocean in the north, and the Indian Ocean in the south. In the east is the Pacific Ocean. The continent of Europe borders the west. It is the biggest of all continents, and also the most populated one. India and China are in Asia. Two out of three people in the world are either Chinese or Indian. Over one billion people live in China. There are more than 50 countries in Asia. Some of them, like Japan and Taiwan, are very wealthy. Others, like Bangladesh and Afghanistan, are very poor.

The Himalayas are Asia's great mountain chain. In this chain is the highest mountain in the world, Mount Everest. It has an

altitude of 8,840 metres. The Earth's lowest depression is also found in Asia. The Dead Sea is 400 metres below sea level.

Most of Asia's rivers originate in the mountains that form the heart of the continent. From there they drain into the Arctic, Pacific and Indian Oceans. Some of the most important rivers are the Ganges in India, the Yang-tze-Kiang in China and the Mekong in Laos. Two large seas, the Caspian Sea and the Black Sea, are also found in Asia.

Asia has a wide variety of climates. North Siberia, in Russia, has a polar climate while most of Southeast Asia has a tropical climate.

Europe

Europe is the smallest and also one of the most diverse continents. It is bordered by the Atlantic Ocean in the west. Asia is in the east. The Mediterranean Sea borders the south, and the Arctic Ocean is in the north. Most of Europe, except the north, has a temperate climate.

Europe's highest mountain chains are the Alps, the Pyrenees, the Caucasus and the Ural Mountains. Except for the Volga and the Danube, European rivers are short; however, they provide an important means of communication.

Europe is split into many small countries.In the south, along the Mediterranean coast, some of the oldest civilizations developed. The Greeks, for example, made incredible advances in our knowledge of the world. In the 15th century, people from some of these countries set out to explore new

The Bay of Bengal, Bangladesh.

Research and make a presentation about two countries from each of the seven continents. After the presentation find out differences and similarities among them.

Locate and find out about Mediterranean countries.

The 14th century cathedral in Barcelona, Spain.

The Alps are Europe's most extensive mountain system.

regions. Spain, England and France colonised many lands. Because of this, they have had a very strong influence in other areas of the world.

Africa

Africa is the second largest continent. It is bordered by the Mediterranean Sea in the north, the Atlantic Ocean in the west, and the Indian Ocean in the east. It is separated from Asia by the man-made Suez Canal.

The giraffe and the zebra are a part of Africa's unique fauna.

Mali is one of the most sparsely settled nations in Africa.

Find out the coordinates of the Sahara Desert. Find out which African countries are bordered by the Sahara.

Name the countries of Africa and their capitals.

In Africa we find the largest desert in the world, the Sahara. Africa also contains the world's longest river, the Nile. This is where Egyptians first built their pyramids thousands of years ago. Mountains are not very high in Africa, but lakes such as Victoria, Chad and Nysa are important. The climate is mostly equatorial and very dry.

Africa is made up of 54 countries. Africa's population density is very low, with only 17 people per square mile. Year after year, severe droughts affect the Central African countries. Many people die because of starvation. Organizations like UNICEF and the World Health Organization work to stop hunger and make parts of Africa safer to live in.

Oceania

Oceania is not a true continent. It is the group of more than 10,000 islands in the South Pacific Ocean. It includes the largest island in the world, Australia. The smaller islands of New Zealand are also in Oceania. Other groups of islands are called archipelagos. They include Melanesia, Micronesia and Polynesia. Most of them were formed by volcanoes.

✎ *Locate the Great Barrier Reef of Australia. Name some of Oceania's island nations.*

Australia and New Zealand are the only developed countries in Oceania. The rest of the nations are very small, both in size and population. Many of the people who live there make their living from tourism.

The largest coral reef in the world, the Great **Barrier Reef**, is in Oceania. It is off the eastern coast of Australia.

The climate of most of Oceania is temperate, but northern Australia has a tropical climate. Oceania's total population is 27 million. Of this, 17 million people live in Australia. More than 3 million people live in New Zealand.

Antarctica's coast has the world's largest populations of marine mammals such as walrusses, seals, penguins and sea lions.

Australia was far away from other lands for millions of years. Because of its isolation, its animals are very different. Australia has unique animals like the koala, the kangaroo and the platypus which are not found anywhere else on the planet.

Antarctica

Antarctica is located at the South Pole. It is a big island, always covered with thick ice. This makes it almost impossible for humans to live there. The population of Antarctica is not permanent. It is made up of biologists, geologists and other scientists of many nationalities who come to study this interesting region.

The ice covering Antarctica is 3,000 metres thick.

Many countries claimed control over Antarctica. But in 1959, and later in 1980, an agreement between many countries was reached. They all agreed to conserve Antarctica's rich resources.

✎✎ *Research the different countries that have permanent stations in Antarctica. Find out why their research is important for humankind.*

Chapter 3
The Hydrosphere

About 70 per cent of the Earth's surface is covered by water. This huge amount of water on Earth is known as the hydrosphere. It includes all the oceans, seas, rivers, lakes, and underground water found on the planet. The hydrosphere is very important. Life as we know it cannot exist without water. The water we use is only a small part of all the water on Earth. Water is so precious that we need to use it wisely.

The oceans make up the greatest part of the hydrosphere. It was in the oceans where life first began to appear on Earth.

The Earth's Oceans

The continents are separated by oceans: the Atlantic, Pacific, Indian, Arctic and Antarctic Oceans. The biggest ocean is the Pacific, which occupies a third of the Earth's surface.

The oceans and the seas are very important to humans. They provide us with food and minerals such as salt. We also use the oceans and seas as highways to move from place to place. The ocean's wealth does not belong to any particular country. It belongs to all living things on Earth. We are all responsible for taking care of it.

Find out about the Earth's oceans and list them from largest to smallest.

Write a short composition about the water cycle.

Find out about the Law of the Sea.

The Water Cycle

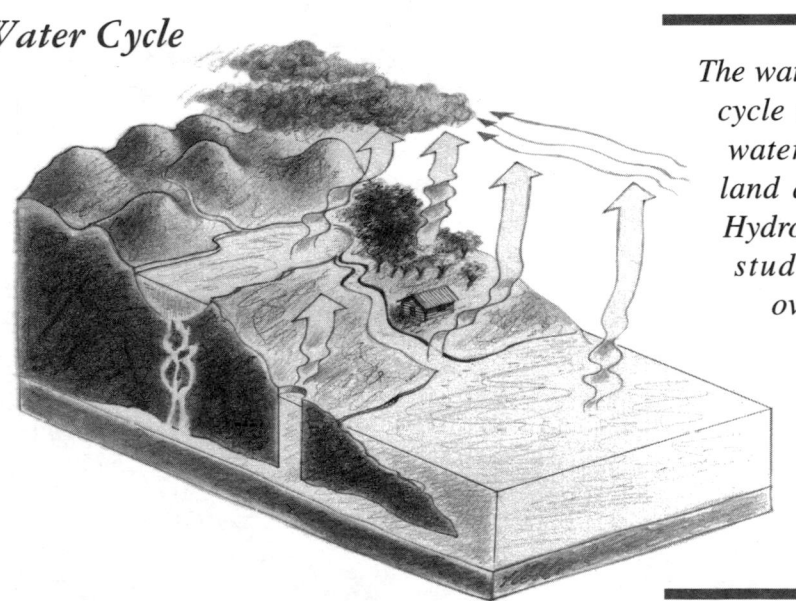

The water cycle or hydrological cycle is the continual flow of water from the ocean to the land and back to the ocean. Hydrology is the science that studies how water moves over and through the land and how it is stored temporarily on or within the Earth.

The Continental Shelf

When you go to the beach, you know that the land under the sea does not drop suddenly. That is because the edges of the continents extend into the oceans. These edges are called continental shelves. These shelves gradually drop to a depth of about 200 metres below sea level.

Look at the physical map on your Atlas of Belize. Note the limits of Belize's continental shelf.

The continental shelves are very important to humans. Great numbers and varieties of fish live and feed there. Reefs like the Belize Barrier Reef are found on the continental shelf.

Write about the importance of the continental shelf for marine life.

Continental shelves are very rich in **plankton**. Plankton are tiny plant and animal organisms. They are the main source of food for the oceans' animals and coral. With so much food and warm temperatures, continental shelves teem with life.

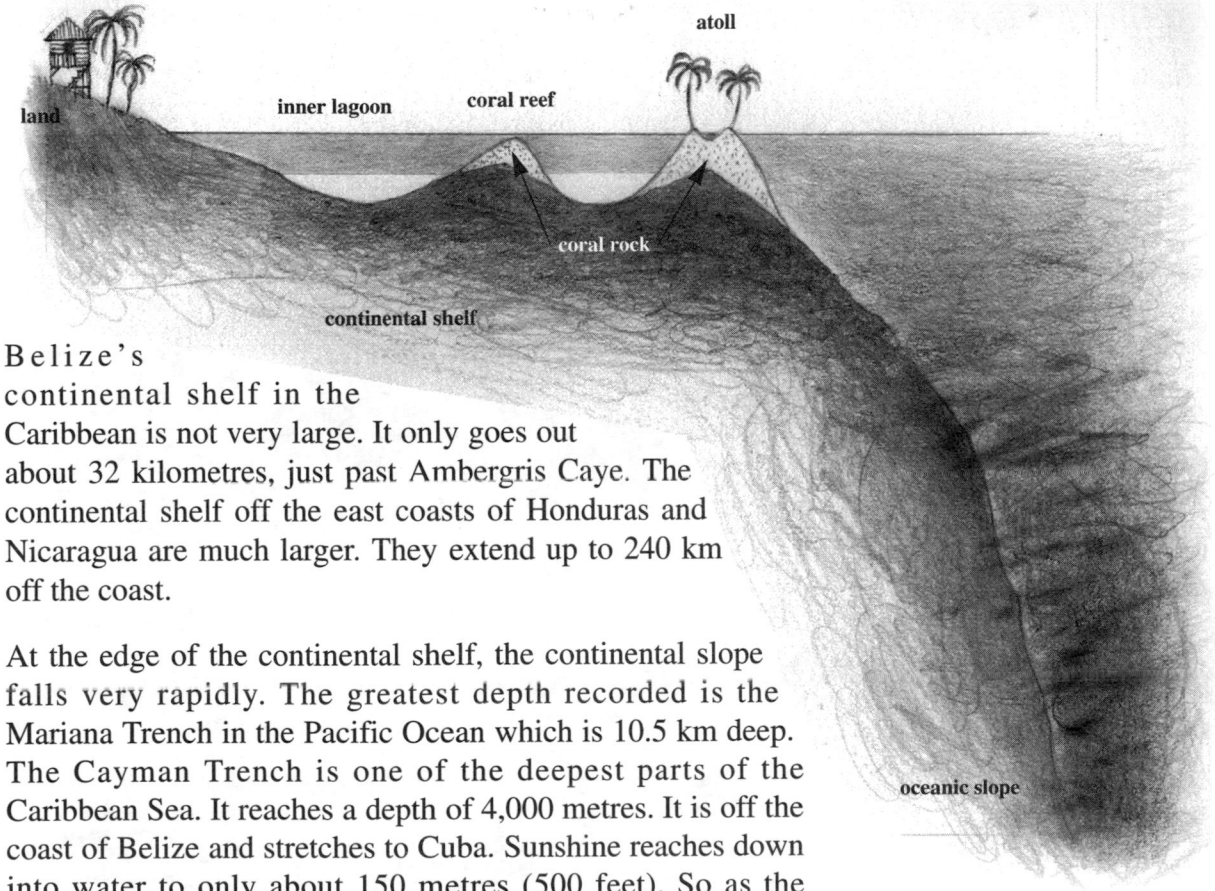

Belize's continental shelf in the Caribbean is not very large. It only goes out about 32 kilometres, just past Ambergris Caye. The continental shelf off the east coasts of Honduras and Nicaragua are much larger. They extend up to 240 km off the coast.

At the edge of the continental shelf, the continental slope falls very rapidly. The greatest depth recorded is the Mariana Trench in the Pacific Ocean which is 10.5 km deep. The Cayman Trench is one of the deepest parts of the Caribbean Sea. It reaches a depth of 4,000 metres. It is off the coast of Belize and stretches to Cuba. Sunshine reaches down into water to only about 150 metres (500 feet). So as the ocean becomes deeper, it also becomes dark and cold.

27

Currents and Tides

Ocean currents are like rivers within the sea. The water flows in the same pattern all the time. Currents are produced by several elements. The temperatures in the water, the prevailing winds and salt content all affect an ocean current.

From ancient times, sailors knew about ocean currents. They used them to travel long distances. Even today, large ships use them to move faster along their routes.

Sea currents have a big influence on climate. Warm sea currents reach the coast and make the climate milder. Other currents move warm water away from the equator. As the current circles, it loses its heat. Then another current will bring cool water back to the equator.

✎ What is the composition of seawater?

✎✎ In the ocean current's diagram, locate the areas where cold and warm currents meet. Note that these are the world's richest fishing grounds.

Ocean Currents

— Warm
----- Cold
◯ Fishing Areas

Ocean currents also affect marine plants and animals. You have read about how plankton is important to life in the ocean. Plankton tends to sink to the bottom of the sea. But the currents' turbulence brings it to the surface again. Plankton can also be carried long distances by ocean currents. Marine animals follow the food as it is moved by the sea.

Listen to the Weather Bureau and make a table recording high tide and low tide for a period of five days.

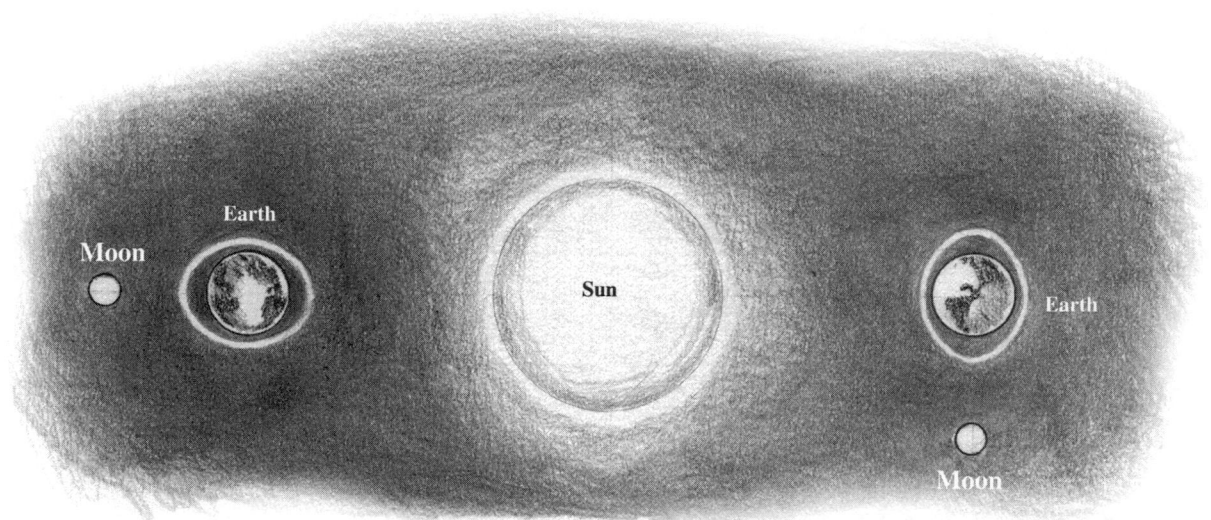

Tides

Tides are the regular rise and fall of the water level in the oceans. This is caused by the gravitational pull of the moon and the sun, and by the Earth's rotation. A complete tide is produced every 12 or 24 hours.

Tides are important because they wash away harmful sediments that accumulate near the shores of the seas and oceans. Also, they provide the right conditions for many species to develop and grow, such as the right temperatures and a quiet environment. For instance, at low tide the water is warmer.

Every day, the Weather Bureau announces at what time the low and high tides will occur. Fishermen listen to the weather report since high tide is a good time to catch fish. Tourist guides taking visitors to the reef also need information about the tides. During high tides sea currents travel from the sea to the coast. But during low tides, the current reverses its direction. Divers, snorkelers or swimmers may be carried out to sea by the current.

The Amazon River is the second longest river in the world.

One of the longest and most important rivers in the world is the Mississippi River in North America.

✎ *Draw a map of Belize and locate and identify Belize's major rivers.*

✎✎ *Find out about some of the world's major rivers and their economic importance.*

Water on Land

Water within the Earth's continents is called continental water. This includes rivers and lakes and, most importantly, underground water.

Water is neither created nor destroyed. It moves around in cycles. We call this movement the water cycle. Water is essential for all life. We can survive without food for many weeks. But after one week without water, we would die.

Continental water makes up only 3 per cent of all water on the planet. Less than half of the Earth's rainfall ends up in the sea. Of the water that falls on the land, some is absorbed by plants. Some filters through the ground into caverns and streams. The rest runs over the surface to form streams and rivers. All the water in rivers eventually reaches a lake, sea, or ocean.

Rivers

A river is a natural stream of water flowing in a channel to the ocean or a lake. The area from which a river collects water is called a catchment, or river basin.

Most rivers form in mountains and hills. The steep drop collects rainwater that runs off the surface of the Earth. It may also collect from underground springs. Some rivers are born from melting glaciers high in the mountains.

Rivers are important for humans for many reasons. Rivers readily provide water for our domestic needs and agriculture. People also use rivers for transportation. In the past, river transport was often the easiest way of travelling to remote places inland.

Ground Water

Rainwater that does not run over the Earth's surface filters underground. There it forms ground water deposits beneath the surface. These deposits provide humans with clean water for domestic use and agriculture.

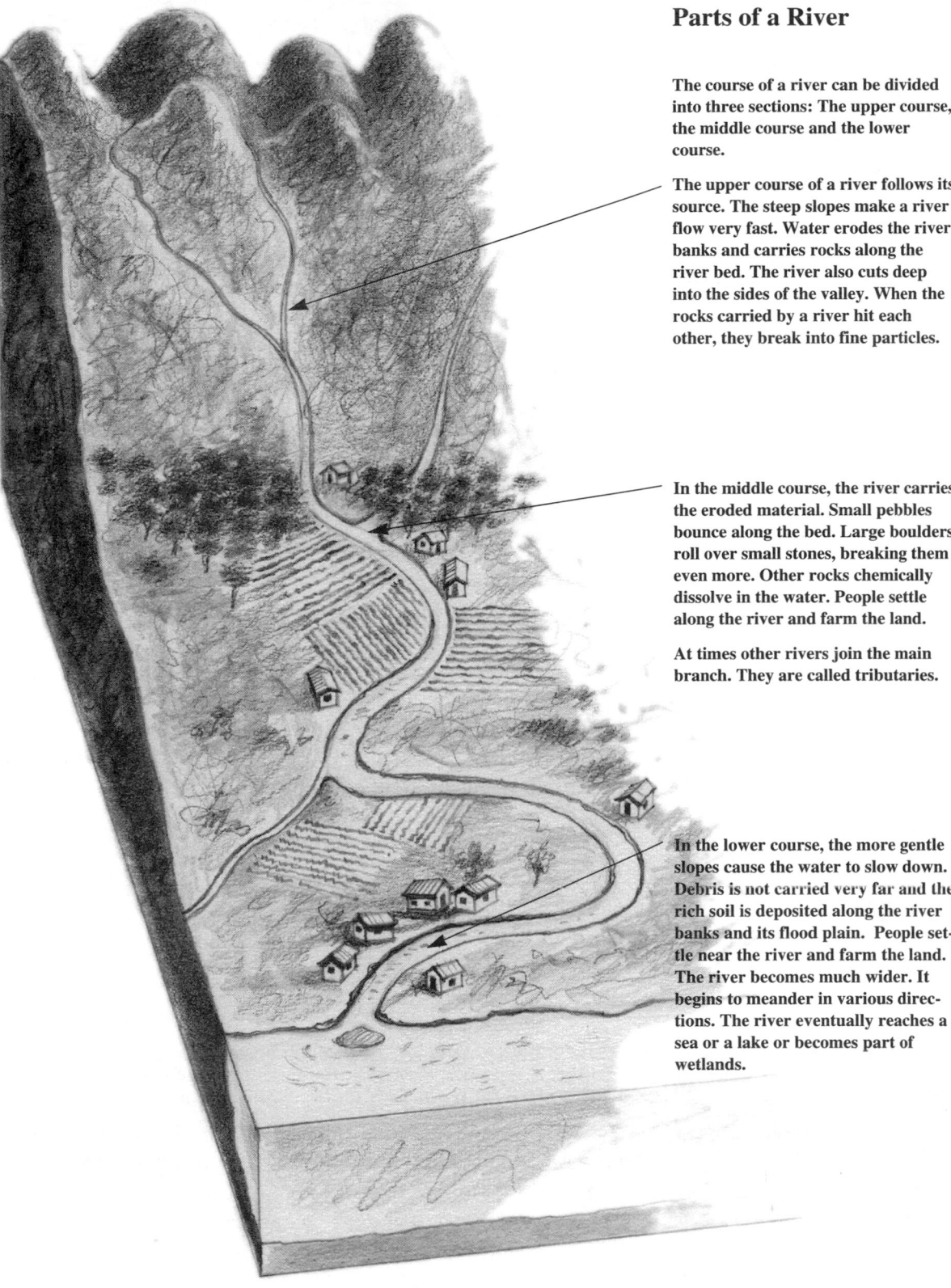

Parts of a River

The course of a river can be divided into three sections: The upper course, the middle course and the lower course.

The upper course of a river follows its source. The steep slopes make a river flow very fast. Water erodes the river banks and carries rocks along the river bed. The river also cuts deep into the sides of the valley. When the rocks carried by a river hit each other, they break into fine particles.

In the middle course, the river carries the eroded material. Small pebbles bounce along the bed. Large boulders roll over small stones, breaking them even more. Other rocks chemically dissolve in the water. People settle along the river and farm the land.

At times other rivers join the main branch. They are called tributaries.

In the lower course, the more gentle slopes cause the water to slow down. Debris is not carried very far and the rich soil is deposited along the river banks and its flood plain. People settle near the river and farm the land. The river becomes much wider. It begins to meander in various directions. The river eventually reaches a sea or a lake or becomes part of wetlands.

Water well, Belize.

pores filled with water and air

saturation zone

well

impermeable rocks

✎ *Find out about the existence of wells in your community and their water table.*

By drilling wells, we can reach underground water. There are still many villages in Belize that rely on wells for their water supply.

The rocks below the Earth's surface hold over 8 million cubic kilometres of water. In the ground, water seeps downward through an aeration zone. Here, the pores in the rocks are filled with a mixture of water and air which help to filter and clean the water.

Below this region, ground water collects in the saturation zone. In this zone the pores are full of water. The boundary between the two zones is called the water table. This is the level of the water surface in wells and boreholes. The height of the water table can vary. This can depend on the amount of rainfall or the amount of water extracted from a well.

Where the surface of the ground meets the water table, water flows as a spring. There are various types of springs. For example, valley springs appear along the lower slopes of valleys where the water table reaches the surface.

Lakes

A lake is a large body of water surrounded by land. It may have collected from rainwater, melting glaciers or rivers. Just like rivers, lakes are important for fishing, agriculture, domestic water supply and transportation. Lakes are also popular as tourist attractions and for water sports. Lakes in Belize are not very large. They are generally near the coast and are called lagoons. Some of Belize's lagoons are Crooked Tree Lagoon, Lamanai and Five Blues Lake.

Five Blues Lake, Belize.

Chapter 4
The Atmosphere

Our planet is surrounded by a layer of gases. They reach from the Earth's surface to a height of about 1,600 kilometres. We call this layer the atmosphere.

The atmosphere is composed of a mixture of gases. They are held in place by the Earth's gravity. The gases contain nitrogen (78 per cent) and oxygen (21 per cent). There is also a little carbon dioxide, and very small quantities of other gases such as argon and helium. Water vapour is also present in the atmosphere. The amount varies from place to place. Without it there would be no rain, snow or fog. In Belize, the amount of water vapour, or humidity, in the air is very high. This gives us plenty of rain and fog.

Deforestation is one of the causes for global climatic changes.

The Atmosphere is Essential for Life on Earth

The atmosphere shields us from the sun's dangerous ultraviolet rays. It protects us against meteorites. Most importantly, it provides us with the oxygen we breathe.

The oxygen in the atmosphere is constantly being renewed. This process is called photosynthesis. Plants take in carbon dioxide, which living organisms give out. They convert it into oxygen. Without photosynthesis, oxygen in the atmosphere would soon be used up. This is why preserving forests is very important. We sometimes call forests the lungs of the Earth.

Smog released from factories causes air pollution.

Humans create a lot of **pollution** from vehicles and factories. We contaminate the air by making large amounts of carbon dioxide. At the same time, deforestation, the cutting down of trees, means there is less oxygen returned to the atmosphere. This is happening all around the globe. It could cause irreparable damage to the atmosphere. This would cause very serious changes to the Earth's climate.

✏️✏️ *Find out about the ozone layer. Research and discuss how human activity may cause climatic changes.*

The Layers of the Atmosphere

The troposphere is the lowest layer of the atmosphere. It varies in depth. It may be less than 10 kilometres deep near

Cumulus clouds.

✎ *Make a list of all the climatic activities in the troposphere.*

✎✎ *Listen to the Belize Weather Bureau. Make charts recording the conditions of the atmosphere for a period of three days. Compare and discuss the findings.*

✎ *Observe cloud formations. Find out the names of the different types of clouds you see for a period of five days.*

the poles, and 16 kilometres deep at the tropics. The highest point of the Earth's surface, Mount Everest at 8,840 metres, extends high into the troposphere.

The troposphere contains about 75 per cent of all the air in the atmosphere. The temperature in the troposphere gets colder by 0.6°C every 100 metres above the Earth. This is why the weather is cooler in the mountainous areas of Belize. The amount of oxygen decreases with altitude. When people climb Mount Everest, they have to wear oxygen masks to help them breathe.

Weather occurs in the troposphere. Clouds, wind and rain all form there. Meteorology is the study of events that take place in the atmosphere. Meteorologists study this phenomena. They make precise measurements of the conditions of the atmosphere. They record things such as water vapour, temperature, air pressure, wind speed and rainfall. Every day meteorologists at the Belize Weather Bureau record the conditions at different points of the country. With the help of **satellite** pictures they can accurately predict the weather. Weather is the condition of the atmosphere at a particular time or over a short period. The average weather that an area experiences over a long period of time is called climate.

Above the troposphere we find the stratosphere. This contains the ozone layer. The ozone protects the planet from the ultraviolet radiation of the sun. In the stratosphere there are no clouds and there is complete stillness. Most jets fly in the lower stratosphere. They have to carry oxygen masks for each passenger. They are used if the airplane cabin loses its pressurised air.

Above the stratosphere we find the mesosphere, the ionosphere and the exosphere.

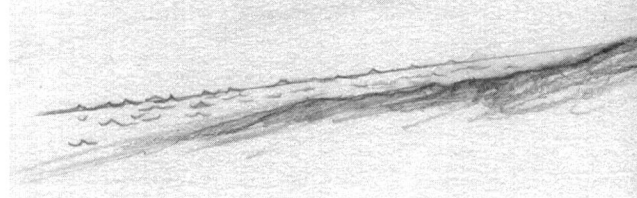

Clouds

Clouds come in many shapes and forms. We give clouds different names depending on their shape, what they are made of, and how high they are above the Earth. Cirrus clouds form at very high altitude. Cumulus clouds have a flat base and great white rounded heaps. Nimbus clouds are dark grey and bring rain.

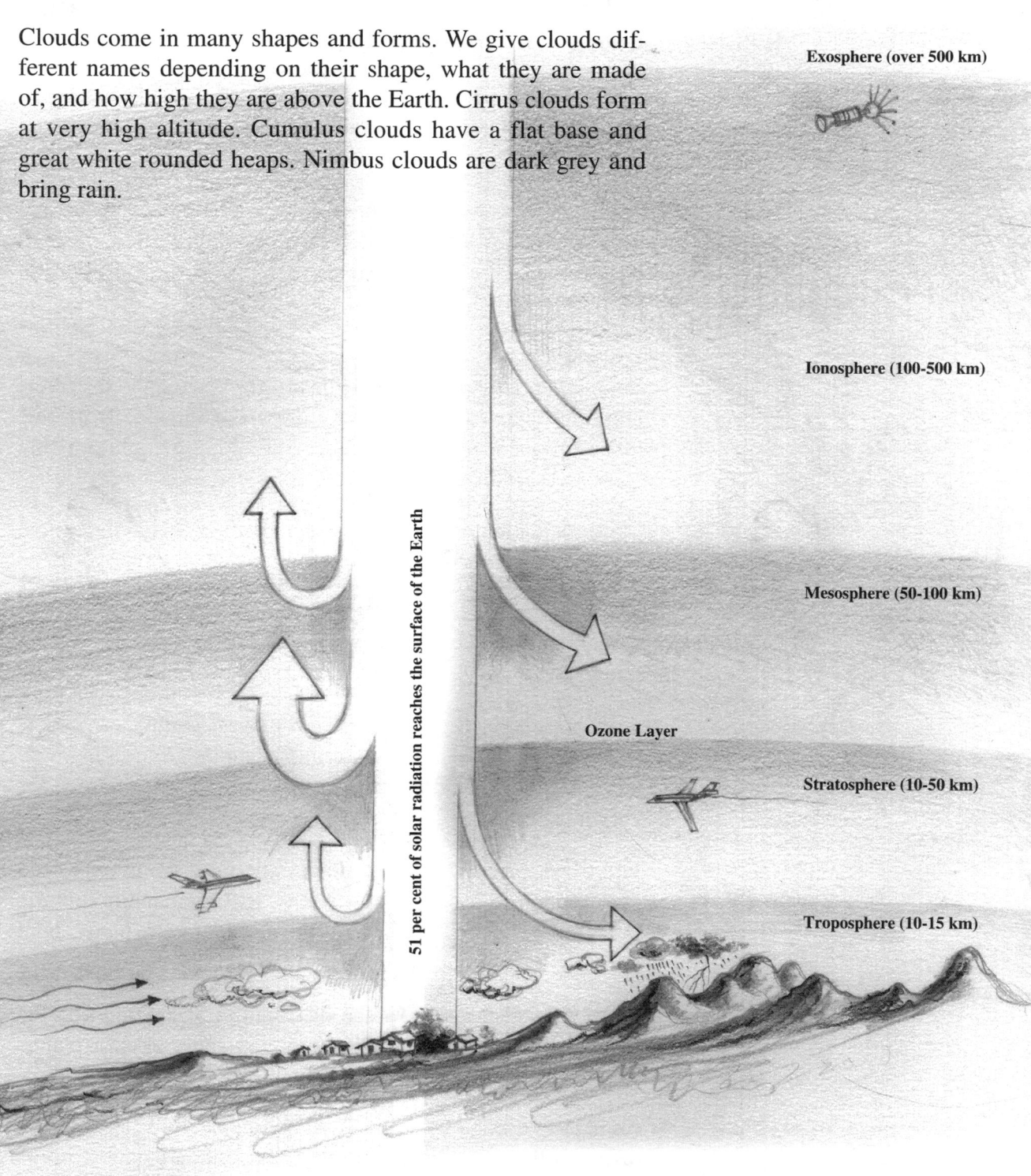

Exosphere (over 500 km)

Ionosphere (100-500 km)

Mesosphere (50-100 km)

Ozone Layer

Stratosphere (10-50 km)

Troposphere (10-15 km)

51 per cent of solar radiation reaches the surface of the Earth

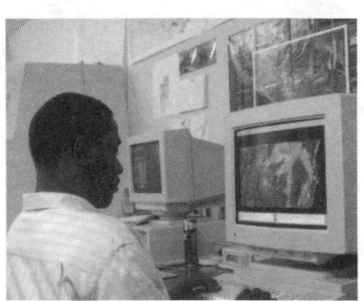

Topographic surveying and satellite images are used to obtain information for maps.

Chapter 5
Understanding Maps

The Earth is best represented by a globe. However, a map, a flat portrait of the Earth, is more practical to use. It is more portable, and less expensive to produce.

A map is the result of an investigation. On maps, we are able to view information globally. Many pages of written information would have to be read to include all the information found on a map. Even then, the information could not be viewed together.

To interpret a map we need to be able to understand the information. We need to be able to draw conclusions from this information. Most important are the map orientation, the scale and the key.

Map orientation tells us where the north is. It is represented by an arrow, or a compass, pointing north.

A scale is the information which tells us the true distance on the ground. Scale can be expressed in one of three ways: fractionally, verbally or graphically.

Symbols are small drawings that represent features. In smaller maps, symbols can stand for important buildings. On larger maps, symbols could be used to show what kinds of crops are grown in a region.

There are a great variety of maps. The most commonly used map types are physical and political. Other maps include topographic maps, geological maps, vegetation maps, land use maps and zoological maps.

Distributional maps show the distribution of anything on the Earth's surface. For example, they can show us at a glance where most people live.

An atlas is a book of maps that may include either a specific region or the entire world. It may also contain thematic information for a region on such topics as climate, geology, vegetation or population.

Explain the three different ways in which scale can be represented in a map.

Research and name the main types of maps.

Draw a map of your neighbourhood, town or village. Use map orientation, a scale and a key.

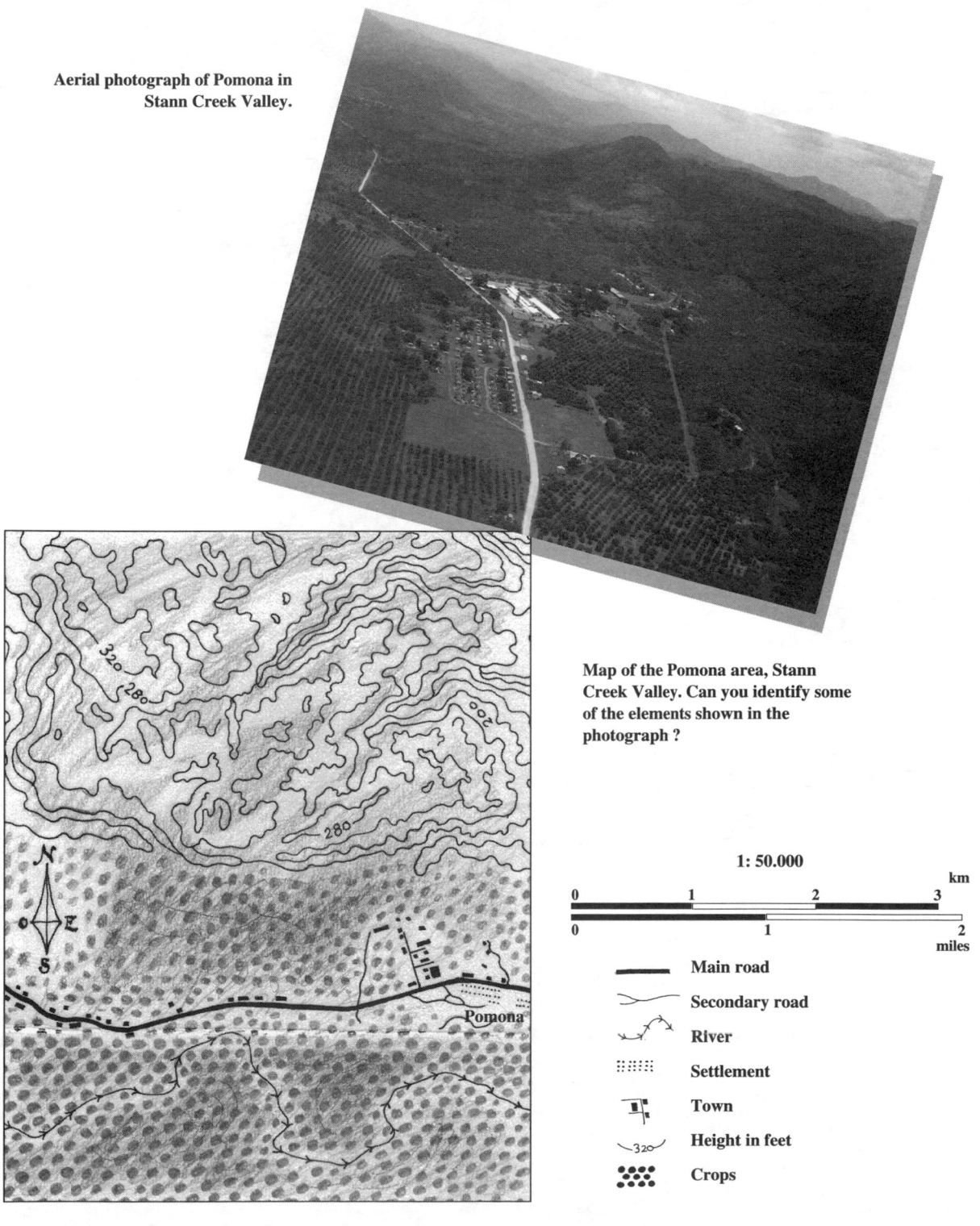

Aerial photograph of Pomona in
Stann Creek Valley.

Map of the Pomona area, Stann
Creek Valley. Can you identify some
of the elements shown in the
photograph ?

Pomona

1: 50.000

			km
0	1	2	3

		miles
0	1	2

——— Main road

⌒ Secondary road

River

⁝⁝⁝⁝⁝ Settlement

Town

⌒320⌒ Height in feet

●●●● Crops

Part Two
Belize: The Land and its People

THE LAND OF BELIZE TODAY is an area as diverse as the people who live there. In this section, we will study the country, from the rocks and minerals beneath its soils to the weather patterns that are created in its skies. We will look at the people who inhabit Belize, who they are and where they came from.

In the following chapters we will study the physical and human geography of Belize and show how the proper use of natural resources can benefit both the land and the people.

The connections between the land and the way people live will become more apparent as we study the way one affects the other.

Millions of years ago, the area of Belize was completely underwater. In this vast ocean, massive underwater explosions of volcanoes formed the first visible land of what would become Central America: the Maya Mountains.

As the volcanoes erupted, they built up cones that rose above the level of the sea. Belize probably began as a series of small volcanic islands. As the Earth's surface continued to evolve, polar ice sheets melted and froze again. When this happened, the ocean rose and fell too. From about 300 million to 248 million years ago, the area of Belize peaked out of the ocean, then was covered again by the sea.

Today, human activity may cause the level of the sea to rise once more. If this were to happen, many of the world's great cities would be covered by the ocean. Unless we change the ways we develop, this could happen as fast as in a generation or two.

The Maya Mountains.

Chapter 6
Geology of Belize

From Volcano to Diverse Country

Belize can be divided into three **geological** areas: the Maya Mountains, Northern Belize and Southern Belize.

The oldest rocks in Belize are of Paleozoic age. These occur in the Maya Mountain region and are referred to as the Santa Rosa Group. The Santa Rosa **metasediments** were deposited as shales, sandstones, limestone and **conglomerates** along with the Bladen Volcanic Member, which is a thick sequence of extrusive volcanic rocks such as rhyolite, pyroclastic rocks and volcanic **sediments**.

The Mountain Pine Ridge, the oldest land surface of Central America.

The Maya Mountains were uplifted in a block towards the end of the Paleozoic era. That push from the Earth gave the mountains enough height to stay above sea-level for 50 million years, during which time rain and wind began to wear down much of the eastern slopes. The northern and southern sides also were affected. Rivers and streams tumbled huge boulders down into valleys.

This **erosion** continued for millions of years, throughout the Triassic period and most of the Jurassic period. The intrusive granite we see today in the Maya Mountain region also formed during the Triassic period.

Start a collection of different rocks that you find from throghout the country and get assistance to identify as many as you can.

In the Cretaceous period that followed, the sea exploded with life. This was due in part to the enrichment of the sea from the weathering of rocks eroded from the Maya Mountains. With abundant food, many new forms of life began to evolve. Many of these tiny organisms had shells. Over millions of years, these shells formed a layer of lime-rich sediments which covered the ocean floor in places to a thickness of about 2,000 metres. During Cretaceous time, much of the land in Belize remained under the sea except for perhaps one period when only the top of the Maya Mountains remained above sea level.

Find out about different agents of erosion. List the effects of erosion on the landscape.

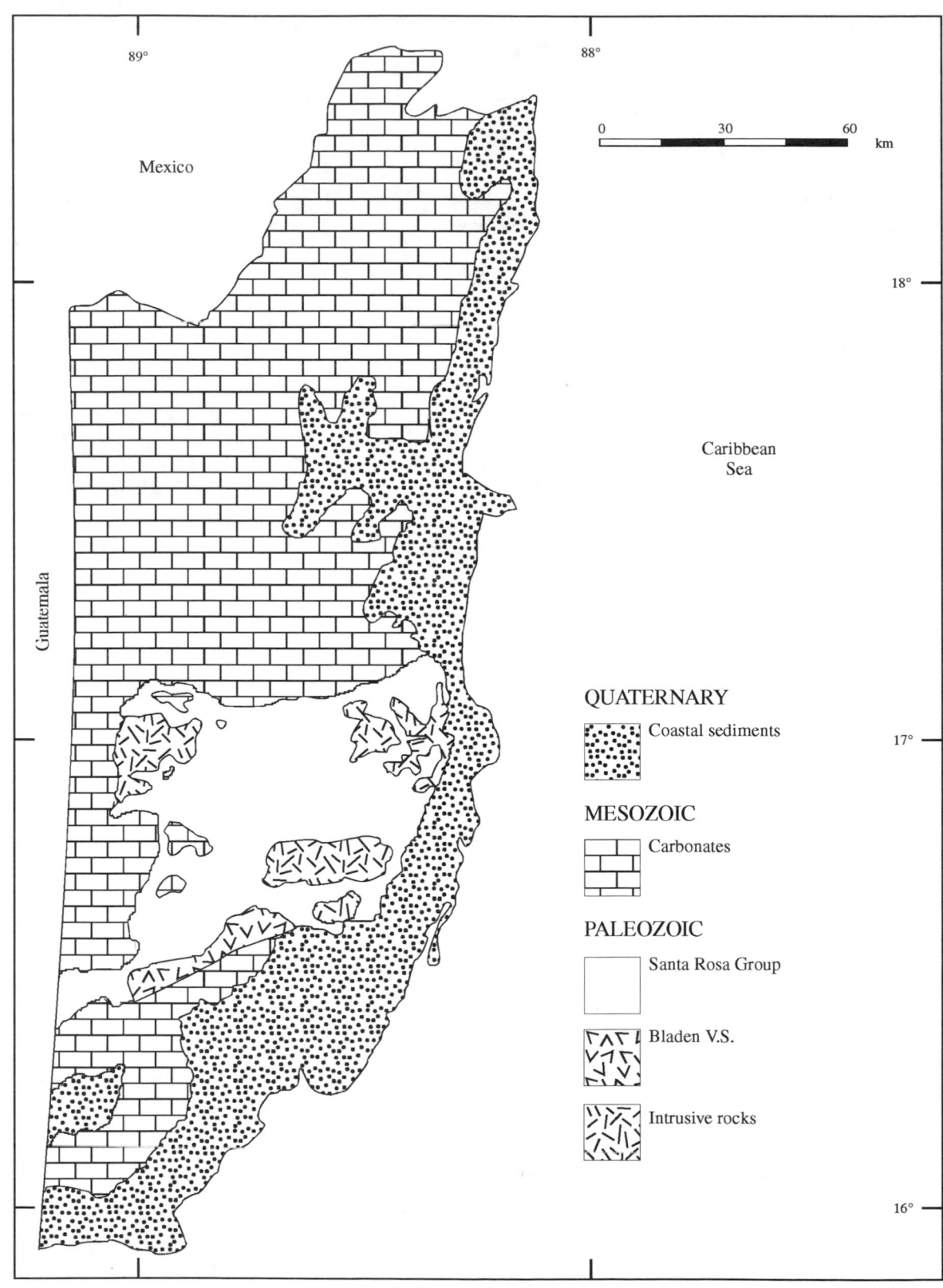

Mexico

Guatemala

Caribbean
Sea

0   30   60
km

QUATERNARY
Coastal sediments

MESOZOIC
Carbonates

PALEOZOIC
Santa Rosa Group

Bladen V.S.

Intrusive rocks

89°   88°   18°   17°   16°

At about the mid-Cretaceous period, renewed movements inside the Earth started again to push up the Maya Mountains, over which limestone was still being deposited. During this earth movement, much of this limestone was broken up and shattered into large blocks. This gave rise to a very porous type of limestone which today has become full of pot holes and caves. This type of landscape is called **karst** landscape.

Minerals and Rocks

Geologists classify rocks according to the way they are formed. There are three kinds of rocks: igneous, sedimentary and metamorphic.

Igneous rocks are formed when molten magma cools and solidifies. They are divided into two groups: intrusive rocks which are formed when magma solidifies beneath the Earth's surface; and extrusive rocks which are formed when magma solidifies above the Earth's surface. Granite and gabbro, for example, are intrusive rocks; basalt and rhyolite are extrusive rocks.

Sedimentary rocks are the most common on the Earth's surface. They are formed by the deposition, compression and cementing together of numerous small particles of mineral, animal or plant origin. Some examples of sedimentary rocks are limestones, sandstones and shales.

Metamorphic rocks occur when rocks are exposed to very high temperatures or pressures, such as when they are buried deep in a mountain range. Regional metamorphic rocks, such as phyllite, schist and slate, are changed by pressure. Thermal metamorphic rocks, such as marble and quartzite, result from the effect of heat.

Most rocks consist of at least two different minerals. Sometimes they contain five or six.

Fossils are impressions of a plant or an animal that existed in the past. Fossils can be of bones, teeth, leaves, wood fragments, shells of animals or even foot imprints. Fossils are found all over the Earth. Through them we have discovered **extinct** animals like dinosaurs, flying reptiles and saber-toothed cats. They are a record of the history of life on the Earth.

The Cayo foothills in the San Antonio area, Cayo District.

What type of alluvial materials were deposited in Belize?

The Cockscomb.

The Maya Mountains were covered with limestone, which erodes quickly. A great amount of limestone, rocks and other materials were swept away by water and wind. These were carried by rivers into the shallow bay at the foot of the mountains. As the mountains crumbled, enormous chunks of limestone broke loose and fell down the mountainsides. Over time, these would become the Cayo foothills.

As the top layer of limestone eroded, some of the original granite rock beneath it was exposed. The Mountain Pine Ridge and the Cockscomb Range areas contain much of this exposed granite.

At one time erosion of the northern flank of the Maya Mountains produced a mixture of white marl, reddish **clay** and sand which accumulated on the northern coastal shelf. At that time it was still partly under a shallow sea.

Many of the rivers at this time were flowing north, following **fault** lines, towards what is known today as the Bay of Corozal. Over the last 65 million years, the shallow ocean waters that covered northern Belize gradually filled with more limestone material until a gently rolling plain was formed. This now comprises Northern Belize.

Southern Belize can be divided into an area of limestone hills and an area where the Toledo beds are exposed.

The limestone rocks form all the hills south of the Maya Mountains and possess typical karstic features. The Toledo beds form a gently rolling plain made of rocks comprising mudstones, sandstones, limestones and **conglomerates**.

Chapter 7
The Belize Landscape

What is a Landscape?

In the last chapter, we studied how Belize's geological history has strongly affected our present landscape. A landscape is an area of the Earth with distinctive topographic features.

A landscape is the result of many natural geological events. Most natural processes like these take millions of years to make changes. Some, like earthquakes, can make large changes overnight.

During the past hundred years, people have been responsible for many changes to the landscape. When we build factories, roads and airports or clear the land for farms, we quickly alter a landscape that may not have changed for centuries. In countries like the U.S., Japan or El Salvador, the impact of large populations has affected the landscape very much.

In Belize, the landscape has changed slowly. This is because our **population density** has been low. Development has been slow and there are still few highways, factories and large farms. We can protect our landscape and use it wisely by learning from the problems other more developed countries experience.

✐✐ *Use clay or other materials to make a model of Belize's landscape showing the Maya Mountains, the coastal plains and the main river valleys.*

✐✐ *Make a list of human-made changes to the landscape. Make another list of natural-made changes to the landscape.*

Human-made changes to the landscape.

Citrus on the slopes of the eastern foothills that border the upper North Stann Creek River Valley.

Rocky Point, Ambergris Caye.

A mangrove caye in Southern Belize.

Crooked Tree Lagoon, Belize District.

Identify in a map Belize's four natural regions.

Belize's Landscape

Belize's landscape is very diverse. Within our 22,962 square kilometres, or 8,866 square miles, there are islands, reefs, coastlines, rivers, lakes, caves, swamps, mountains, hills and forests. Because it lies north of the Tropic of Capricorn and just south of the Tropic of Cancer, Belize is just within the category of a tropical country. However, because it lies so close to the northern limit of the tropics it is usually referred to as a subtropical country.

Our country lies on the Caribbean seacoast of Central America, about 965 kilometres west of Jamaica. To the north lies Mexico's Yucatan **Peninsula**, and to the west and south lie Guatemala and the Gulf of Honduras. The mainland extends 280 kilometres (174 miles) from the Rio Hondo in the north to the Sarstoon River in the south. At its widest point, Belize measures 109 kilometres (68 miles) from east to west.

We can divide the country into four regions. These are Northern Belize, the Maya Mountains, Southern Belize and the Coastal Zone.

Northern Belize

Northern Belize is the region lying north of the Maya Mountains. In this region there are two ranges of limestone hills and a large plain extending north and east. One limestone range stretches along the western border from the Yalbac hills to Blue Creek. The other limestone range is between the Western Highway and the Maya Mountains.

Between the hills in these regions, flat lands have built up from the clays and sands brought by the rivers coming down the Maya Mountains. The main plain is a wide stretch of flat land, with a large area of swamps and marshes only a few feet above sea level. As we have seen in the previous chapter, this area was once a shallow sea.

Pine forests are abundant in the region. Northern Belize produces most of the sugar cane grown in the country, as well as crops like corn and beans.

In the north, large rivers such as the Hondo and New River flow from the Yalbac Hills towards Chetumal Bay. Some, like the Belize and Sibun Rivers, begin in the Maya Mountains in the Cayo District. The rivers pass through the districts of Cayo, Belize, Orange Walk and Corozal. The Rio Hondo, the New River and the Sibun River are the longest rivers in Belize.

Rivers in this region often run in straight lines, following geological faults in the ground. They flow slowly due to the lack of gradient.

In the ancient past, many rivers in this region followed different courses than they do today. Geologists find terraces where rivers left deposits of sands, clays and flint pebbles. When these rivers abandoned their usual course, they left behind hollowed out areas that filled with water and became lagoons.

The Maya Mountains

The mountainous region in the south-central part of the country is known as the Maya Mountains. They rise to over 914 metres and are covered with mixed hardwood forest. One of the highest peaks is Victoria Peak (1,121 m or 3,680 ft) in the Cockscomb Range.

The Mountain Pine Ridge is the oldest land surface in Central America. It is part of the remains of an ancient island since during the Cretaceous Period a part of the Maya Mountains may have been above the level of the ocean.

The Cockscomb Range contains Belize's highest peaks. The hills are formed by quartzite, a hard rock that resists erosion.

In the Mountain Pine Ridge, the Cockscomb region and the Hummingbird-Mullins River regions, the rock is mostly granite. The southern part of the mountains includes a belt of volcanic rocks formed from lava and ash. This belt runs from Little Quartz Ridge in the west to the Bladen Branch of the Monkey River and the Trio Branch in the east.

Another dominant feature of the Maya Mountains are the Bald Hills like Baldy Sibun and Baldy Beacon. These hills are bare of vegetation except for grass and sedges.

The Maya Mountains.

The Macal River, Cayo District.

Lowland Pine Ridge landscape, Belize District.

✎ *Follow the course of the Rio Hondo and the New River.*

✎ *In your atlas, locate the Maya Mountains, the Mountain Pine Ridge and the Cockscomb Range.*

From the Maya Mountains, the land slopes in two directions: towards the north and south-east. Many of Belize's rivers have their source in this region.

At the northern base of the Mountain Pine Ridge a series of rivers falls from the ridge only to sink in the limestone karst at its base. Only a few rivers, such as Roaring Creek and Barton Creek, actually make it to the Belize River from where they flow to the sea.

In the Rio On, water erosion has dissolved the limestone revealing the granitic rock.

A classic example of limestone dissolution: the Puente Natural.

Southern Belize

In Southern Belize, which includes parts of the Cayo and all of the Toledo and Stann Creek districts, the landscape contains mountains, hills and plains. This landscape was created from limestone formed during the Cretaceous Period.

Throughout the Toledo region, formations called the Toledo beds were laid down above the limestone. These form the gently rolling plains of the area. In the hills, south of the Maya Mountains, the karst landscape formed by limestone has left a dense network of sinkholes and caves inside the earth. In this area the wetter climate produces a denser rain forest.

In the south-east of the Maya Mountains, shorter rivers spill quickly into the Stann Creek and Toledo districts, emptying into the sea.

The Toledo District is in a unique area of the world. It lies on the southern boundary of a huge tectonic plate, the North

✐✐ Read page 49. Describe how caves are formed.

✐✐ Find in your atlas some of the important rivers that have their source in the south eastern slopes of the Maya Mountains.

Karst Landscape: Deep Caves, Hidden Treasures

Limestone contains minute cracks through which water trickles downward, gradually enlarging them by solution. In time, so much of the rock is dissolved that a network of caverns, sinkholes and underground tunnels develops. The result is called a karst landscape.

Huge networks of caverns can be found all around the limestone of the Maya Mountains. The most extensive cave system is found in the Chiquibul region, one of the five largest natural caverns in the world. Inside the cave, a river disappears for dozens of kilometres, flowing through huge passages and chambers. These enormous caves are often as big as 300 metres by 400 metres and 80 metres high. A few kilometres upstream, an eroded cave forms a large arch, called Puente Natural. In some places, like Rio Frio Cave, the limestone is dissolved all the way to the granite basement. The entrance to this cave is 20 metres high.

When the weight of the ground above a cave cannot be supported, the ceiling collapses and causes huge hollows in the earth called sinkholes. These are usually round with steep cliffs rising several hundred metres. Such features can be seen around the Santa Familia, Caves Branch and Chiquibul regions, as well as around Rio Grande. Another type of sinkhole, often found in Mexico's Yucatan Peninsula, has a deep vertical shaft that is filled with water. These are called cenotes.

From ancient times, caves have been used as shelters by both humans and animals. They have also been used for religious rituals and burials. Because deep caves experience very few changes in weather, bones and other materials are often well preserved. This makes caves very important places for archaeologists to study our history. In caves in Belize, archaeologists have found skeletons, pottery and paintings from the ancient Maya. They have also found fossils of extinct species that were previously unknown to science.

The Barrier Reef and Inner Lagoon.

Mangrove destruction near Belize City.

In your atlas, locate the areas that make up the Coastal Zone.

American Plate, that stretches from Alaska to southern Belize. As we have seen, wherever two tectonic plates meet, there is much geological activity. This activity is the major cause of earthquakes in Guatemala.

The Coastal Zone

Belize's coast runs 280 kilometres, or 174 miles, along the Caribbean Sea. When we talk of a coastal zone, we include the old coastal terraces, the low plain along Belize's coast, the inner lagoon, the Barrier Reef, as well as the hundreds of islands off Belize's coast, and three **atolls**: Lighthouse Reef, Glovers' Reef and Turneffe Islands. The region covers over 23,000 square kilometres. The whole region is particularly susceptible to hurricanes and tropical storms.

The coastal deposits are more developed in Southern Belize and date from the quaternary period when the sea level was 55 metres higher than today. At that time, rivers draining from the Maya Mountains were depositing large amounts of boulders, gravels, flint pebbles and clays in the shallow sea occupying the eastern side of the mountains. Another shore-line with terraces can still be seen in some places at about 15 metres above sea-level. Those quaternary **alluvial** fans have fairly poor soils supporting pine-grass savanna.

Rivers like the Rio Hondo and the New River still carry **sediment** into the Corozal Bay. Nearer to Belize City, the

Point Placencia.

Northern, Belize and Sibun rivers empty into the channel between the mainland and the Barrier Reef.

The sediments from these rivers, along with the mangrove fringe, have created a swampy coastal area. There are also many shallow lagoons of fresh and brackish water.

Mangroves protect the coast from erosion.

Along the southern coastline, the land near the sea becomes more sandy. This is because the sediment from the rivers in these areas comes from the granite mountains. Towns like Dangriga and Hopkins are built on these sandy areas. Some of the best beaches in Belize are found along the Placencia Peninsula.

Rivers like the Mullins, Stann Creek and the Sittee flow through ridges with pine trees. Further south in the Toledo District, rivers like the Rio Grande, Moho and Sarstoon tumble down from the Maya Mountains. They run through **broadleaf** forests before they empty into the Gulf of Honduras.

Belize's southern coast in the vicinity of Punta Gorda.

All along the coast, mangrove trees grow in swamps. The mangrove trees are very important to the health of the coastline. They can grow in salty water, and their roots stop erosion by trapping sediment so that it can not be washed away. The mangroves also provide a rich environment for life in the sea, and many fish use the safety they provide for breeding grounds.

The Barrier Reef, the Inner Channel and Cayes in Belize

A barrier reef is one of the richest **ecosystems** on the Earth. The food and shelter it provides support a wide variety of sea life, from plants and tiny fishes to sharks. Reefs also help to protect the mainland from the devastation of hurricanes.

The Barrier Reef of Belize is 281 kilometres long. This makes it the second longest reef in the world after the Great Barrier Reef of Queensland, Australia, which is more than 1,930 kilometres long. Reefs not only provide a home for plants and animals, but are also very important to the fishing and tourism industries.

In between the Barrier Reef and the mainland coast is the Inner Channel. In the northern section of the channel from Corozal Bay to Belize City, the distance between the coast and the Barrier Reef averages about 20 kilometres. The water is not very deep, usually measuring only 3 to 12 metres.

Which rivers are responsible for the sandy beaches of Belize's southern coast.

Look at the physical map of the atlas. Find the distance from the mainland to the reef in four different points of Belize's coast. Locate the farthest and closest points of the Barrier Reef in relation to the coast.

Reefs can grow until they rise above the water and form a small flat island.

South of Belize City, the distance increases between the mainland and the reef, up to 40 kilometres. The depth of the water also increases, to up to 65 metres. Throughout the channel, the bottom of the lagoon is flat and covered with sea grass, sand and patch reefs. Sediments from rivers combine with coral sediment to cover the bottom.

Coral Reefs and Islands

Look at the photograph on this page. Describe the formation of a coral island.

Unlike the mainland of Belize, which was formed through violent movements of the Earth, the reef and islands of Belize were created from the slow build-up of tiny animals. These animals are called corals. Throughout their life, they remain fixed to the same spot. With a hard shell of calcite, they reproduce by the thousands, forming a colony. Each colony is built up on the rocky skeletons of each coral. This coral mass grows and spreads in shallow offshore water, often around islands. Eventually it forms a narrow area of high ground called a reef.

Coral islands are usually covered with white sand. This sand comes from the eroded material of coral skeletons. In the lagoon behind the reef, there may be boulders of coral material that have been torn off the reef. The water in a lagoon is shallow and its floor is covered by layers of broken coral. This area is known as a reef flat.

There are three main types of reefs. A fringing reef forms a shelf around an island, just below water level. A barrier reef lies at a distance from an island or coast, forming a rough ring or line. It is separated from the land by a shallow lagoon. An atoll is a round formation of coral islands, the remainders of a reef that once surrounded a volcanic island.

There are approximately 450 cayes along and within the Belize Barrier Reef. Many of them are very tiny and unable to support settlements. Most islands with settlements are north of Belize City. Ambergris Caye is the largest and most populated. Other important islands are Caye Caulker, Caye Chapel and St. George's Caye in the north, and Southwater Caye and Tobacco Caye in the south. Together, the islands make up 689 square kilometres of land.

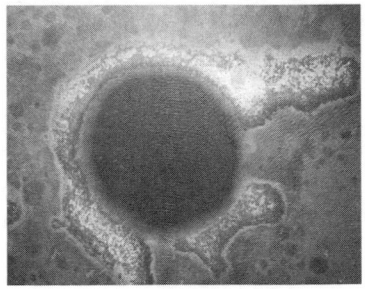

The Blue Hole sinkhole at Lighthouse Atoll.

The Offshore Atolls

There are three atolls outside the Barrier Reef. They are Turneffe Islands, Lighthouse and Glovers' reefs. They are very remote and isolated, but they are frequently used for scientific research stations and as diving sites. Because of this, each atoll has resorts. Their economy also depends on tourism and fishing.

Turneffe Islands are covered largely with mangroves. Half Moon Caye Natural Monument is found at Lighthouse Atoll, and covers a part of the reef and inner lagoon.

Find the coordinates of some of the islands that support populations.

On a map, locate each of Belize's atolls. List each of the atolls' main physical features.

Half Moon Caye Natural Monument.

Chapter 8
Soils of Belize and their Vegetation

Where Life Begins

Draw a diagram to show how plants get nutrients and water from the soil.

Explain how a soil erodes and what happens when steep slopes are cleared from their original forests.

In groups, discuss how the parent rock, climate and time influences the soil formed. Discuss how the soil determine the vegetation that grows.

There are only a few things on the Earth which can grow on bare rock, like moss and epiphytes. Most plants and other living things require a soil environment in which to grow. The soil provides nutrients and moisture for their growth.

Soils develop, over hundreds of years, from the decomposition of the rocks found in the landscape. Water is a key element in the soil formation process and helps to promote the physical, chemical and biological decay of the rocks to produce soil.

The rocks from which a soil develops are important in determining the nature and property of the soil formed. Other factors like climate and vegetation also influence soil development. On the other hand, the type of vegetation that grows in an area is largely determined by the soil.

It is important that we know our soil resources. In 1954, Belize was the first tropical country to have a complete report done on its soils, ecology and potential land use. More recently, land resource assessments were completed for the entire country and a soil classification system was refined for Belize.

High terraces of the Sibun flood plain are highly suitable for citrus. The Sleeping Giant of the Maya Mountains rests in the background.

The absence of dense forest on the Cockscomb is not unexpected given the infertility of the soils.

The Four Soil Zones

The soils of Belize can be broadly divided into four zones. Zone One contains the soils of the Maya Mountains. Zone Two contains the soils developed from limestone rocks. Zone Three contains soils of the Toledo beds and Zone Four includes soils of the alluvial plains, lowlands and coastal plains.

While we divide the soils of Belize into four categories, in reality there are many different types of soils within each group.

Zone One
A Sparse Land: The Maya Mountains

The land of the Maya Mountains is dominated by steep slopes, with very shallow and stony soils. Few areas of flatter terrain are found in the higher elevations. Once part of an ancient highland **plateau**, the soils in this area may be the oldest in Central America. The soils are very **acidic** with low levels of available nutrients for plants.

Describe soils of Zone One and suggest reasons why much of the Maya Mountains are protected areas.

The predominant vegetation of the area includes a rare palm, epiphytes and other species never before recorded in Belize.

In the other steep areas of the Maya Mountains soils are formed from ancient Paleozoic volcanic and metamorphic rocks. These

55

The depth of soil over limestone rock can vary widely over short distances. Here it varies from 15 to 25 cm.

Discuss why soils of the northern plains would not be easily eroded.

Describe the soils of Zone Two. What makes these soils good for growing sugar cane, corn and beans?

Describe three types of soils in your area and the crops that grow on them.

Once cleared of vegetation, it is difficult to establish trees on the shallow soils of the limestone hills.

soils are also very acidic and lacking in nutrients. Some of the soils are also highly erodible. Despite the harsh conditions, the environment developed a normal forest cover. Most of these soils will never be able to sustain any form of agriculture.

Zone Two
A Delicate Balance: Limestone Soils

Soils derived from limestone rocks cover more than half of the land in Belize. They extend from the dry north to the wet south. The limestone landscape ranges from rugged, hilly and karstic land, steep and rocky slopes to areas of flat, undulating and rolling hills. The rolling hills have the deepest soils, but the majority of limestone soils are shallow and stony.

Black, dark gray-brown or brown in colour, the soils are clay textures with a **neutral** to **alkaline** reaction. The natural vegetation is a mixed broadleaf forest, which efficiently extracts nutrients from the decomposing surface of the limestone rock. The trees then return some of this fertility to the thin soil when their leaves drop and decay.

When dry, these soils have a strong granular structure. But when wet, they become a very heavy, sticky clay. The clay can absorb large quantities of water without runoff. This results in low levels of erosion even when the forest cover is removed. In karstic areas rainfall is absorbed into the limestone, from where it continues down into underground caves and old stream tunnels.

The limestone soils of Zone Two are among the most fertile soils in Belize, containing moderate to ample levels of most plant nutrients. They are important agricultural soils and are the best soils for growing sugar, corn, beans, pasture and many other valuable crops. Many native fruit tree crops like avocado, chicozapote and mammey apple also do well. These soils are also good for plantations of timber-producing trees, such as mahogany, cedar and many other species. In damp flat locations they can grow very good rain-fed rice crops.

The nutrient-rich soils of the northern plains support good crops of sugar cane.

Zone Three
Part Time Use: Toledo Soils

These soils are mainly found on the undulating to rolling lands of the Toledo District. Originally, when they were in

Farmer Knows Best

Soil scientists in Belize are often surprised at the variety of soils in the country. One scientist studied the soil of a farmer whose field was only 3/4 of an acre large. On it he found 18 different types of soil.

Because the farmer had already worked the land for so many years, he knew all the types of soils, and understood what he could grow where and what he could not.

It is because soils in Belize are so variable, even over short distances, that large plots of land for producing one crop often fail. Each type of soil may have differing nutrient contents and drainage needs. Because there are so many different types of soil in a small area, the small farmer usually does better. Even then, he may have to be able to identify 18 types of soil!

🖊 *What are the main properties of the soils in Zone Three?*

🖊🖊 *What is shifting agriculture as practiced by the Maya of Toledo? How does it help to improve soil conditions and increase deforestation?*

their heavily forested conditions, these soils developed from mudstones, siltstones and sandstones. These rocks where laid down over older limestone rocks when southern Toledo was invaded by a shallow sea.

The soils that develop are diverse but are fairly shallow, brown clays and **loams** of moderate acidity and of good fertility. Traditionally, these soils have a reputation for being good agricultural soils. But after 20 to 40 years of continuous farming, they have deteriorated. The soils are mainly clays with weak structure which degrade when used for arable crops and pasture. When trees are cut down the stabilising influence of the

The porous and friable soils of the Toledo uplands are suited to cacao production.

Milpa corn cultivation is a common feature of the Toledo upland landscape.

forest litter is lost. Fine particles from the topsoil move into the subsoil where they block the pores and reduce **soil aeration**. Crop roots need this air in order to feed properly.

Farmers only improve their harvest temporarily by ploughing or adding artificial fertilizers. Tree crops do well on these soils. Citrus, cacao, mango and nutmeg provide more stability for the soil. Many farmers on these soils have found the methods of the ancient Maya to be most effective for producing cash crops in these soils. After a few crops the Maya allowed the forest to regrow in the fields for a few years before using them again. Rice cultivation does very well on these soils but farmers have to contend with serious invasion by weeds.

Zone Four
Swampy and Salty: Lowland Soils

All of the soils in this group are derived from alluvial material carried in rivers, streams or the sea. They are not derived from, nor influenced, by the rocks upon which they are deposited. These soils are located on flat to gently undulating areas of the landscape.

These soils are predominant in the lower part of the Belize River Valley, most of the coast extending along the south of the country and the islands off the Belize shore.

The deposits produce a wide range of soils. They include Belize's most productive agricultural soils, occurring in rivers, valleys and terraces south of the Belize River Valley. Though limited in acreage, they are of significant agricultural value, producing most of Belize's citrus and bananas.

The main soils of the lowland areas are the Pine Ridge soils found in the old coastal plain. These soils are very infertile, with shallow topsoil overlying compact, mottled and wet subsoils. Although extensive in area, these soils have very limited agricultural value.

Along the coast and cayes, many soils have high salt contents which make farming difficult.

Despite these problems, the lowlands still produce many crops. Usually farmers have to use fertilizers or drain areas that have excess water in them. After this is done, some types of soils can grow cashew, rice and corn. Along the coast and on the islands, farmers harvest coconuts, and villagers grow cassava, sweet potatoes, yams and pineapples. Fruit trees like mangoes also can grow here.

In some coastal swamps, logwood used to flourish. This tree was logged by the early settlers of Belize and played an important role in the settlement of our nation. Today, much of the logwood that once grew on these swampy soils has been cut down and low forest and bushes grow in its place.

✎✎ *Look at the agricultural potential map of the atlas. Can you identify areas with alluvial soils?*

✎✎ *Make a chart comparing the main characteristics of Belize's four soil zones.*

Mechanized bean production on gently undulating lands of the northern plains.

Plantains and bananas are well suited to the deep, well drained alluvial valleys.

The mouth of the Monkey River at the Caribbean Sea.

Chapter 9
Rivers and Underground Water

Belize enjoys the benefits – and sometimes the dangers – of many rivers and streams, from north to south. The most important use of rivers in Belize is for domestic water supplies. Rivers are also used for electric power generation, irrigation of farms and industrial processing. Settlements along rivers enjoy them for swimming, as well as transportation.

When we studied rivers in Part 1, we learned that most rivers start in highlands and drain down into lakes or seas. The Maya Mountains have dominated much of the geographic history of Belize; they have been a major influence in determining our present pattern of rivers and streams.

In Cretaceous times, major rivers probably flowed westwards from the highlands towards Guatemala. Then came a time when faulted cracks diverted some of the drainage – rivers were forced to drain into the northern lowlands and out into the Bay of Chetumal.

Later, with the development of the Belize River, some of these northward-flowing rivers changed course and flowed

Define the parts of a river.

List the advantages and disadvantages of living near rivers.

Refer to the clay model of Belize. Use a watering can to simulate rain over the Maya Mountains. Observe how rivers are formed.

eastwards into the Caribbean Sea. Today, when the Belize River has a "top gallon" flood, some of the excess water still flows back into the old northward-draining streams.

Rivers are most important in shaping the landscape. The energy of the river cuts through the mountains and deposits sediments along the banks and in the river valleys near to the coast. Over centuries, the sea level may change and increase the length of the river.

The Rio Hondo forms the northern border of Belize with Mexico. The southern border of Belize follows the twists of the Sarstoon River.

River systems in Belize can be classified in three zones: a source region, a middle region and a lowland region.

Small falls in the Rio On created by the erosion of limestone rocks.

Source Region: Where Rivers Begin

This zone is characterized by steep slopes and swiftly flowing waters. The source region is usually in an area of high rainfall.

The main source region in Belize is the Maya Mountains. If we look at a map of Belize, we can see a dense network of many rivers in the south-east and eastern slopes of the Maya Mountains. Here, water courses flow down the granite hill sides in steep and relatively straight lines, eager to reach the sea. The main rivers that drain this area are North Stann Creek River, Sittee River, South Stann Creek River, Monkey River and Deep River.

Another dense network of river channels covers the western slopes of the Maya Mountains. The Macal River and its tributaries drain the region. In the extreme south of the Toledo District the Rio Grande, Moho River and the Sarstoon River originate from limestone on the southern slopes of the Maya Mountains.

Another source region in Belize is the Yalbac Hills. There we find the sources of the Booth River and the Rio Bravo.

Look at the physical map of the atlas. Trace the old northward course of the Belize River.

Follow the course of the rivers whose source is in the south eastern and eastern slopes of the Maya Mountains.

Swift flow of a small stream high up in the Mountain Pine Ridge area.

The Middle Region: Where Most Food is Grown

This region corresponds to the middle course of most rivers. Here we find more gentle slopes. Thick soils in the river basin have been built up from river sediments and a good flow is maintained in the dry season.

The Belize River, New River and the Rio Hondo in the north and the Stann Creek, Moho, Sarstoon and Temash rivers in the south are good examples of rivers with a well developed middle region. Much of the agricultural activity in Belize occurs in the river valleys of the middle region where the rich soils and abundant water make agriculture successful.

The middle regions are also affected by extreme floods. After heavy rains, flood waters carry sediment over the banks and into the wide river valleys. When the flood waters subside the sediments remain as new soil. This is extremely important for the development of agricultural areas. On the other hand, existing agricultural crops are destroyed or buried by these floods.

The Lowland Region: Where the River Meets the Sea

In this region the rivers run through very flat land with little energy. Rivers meander through this region forming bows and lagoons before discharging into the sea.

Use the physical map of the atlas to locate Belize's main river valleys.

Explain why sediment is important for agriculture.

Where mangrove forests are prevalent the sediments form deltas along the coastline. Tides periodically bring salt sea water to mix in this low region, creating brackish water where marine life can develop and grow. Many fish go up the river deltas to spawn. The right temperature, the quiet waters and the brackish mixtures provide the ideal environment for many fish species to reproduce and grow.

Belize's Major Rivers

In the northern part of Belize, the Rio Hondo, New River and the Belize River are most important. The Rio Hondo defines the boundaries between Belize and Mexico. The New River acts as a transportation route for the sugar industry. It is also used in sugar cane processing, sometimes creating environmental problems.

Belize City grew at the mouth of the Belize River.

The Belize River is the longest river in Belize. Part of the water in the Belize River comes from the Macal River which drains from the Vaca-Chiquibul limestone plateau. Near the town of San Ignacio, the Mopan and the Macal rivers join. From this confluence the Belize River flows eastward to the sea.

When the Belize River begins just north of San Ignacio, it twists and turns eastward toward Crooked Tree. In the ancient past, the Belize River may have kept on flowing north to join the New River. But today it dips south-east at Grace Bank, and finally drains into the sea north of Belize City. Isolated parts of the old Belize River bed form the Crooked Tree and Revenge Lagoon system.

Fill a bottle with flood water. Let it settle. Measure the sediment. Compare the amount of sediment from various other sources.

The Belize River Valley is one of Belize's most active agricultural regions. Most of our rice, beans, corn, potatoes and other food crops are grown there. Belize City, the country's centre of economic activity, is located at the mouth of the Belize River. The country of Belize was named after this important river.

Find out what is a meander and a river delta. Make a diagram of a delta.

The Belize River carries the largest amount of water in the country, nearly 27 per cent of the total drainage. The 194 km stretch of the river was, until about 1950, used as the main method of transportation from Belize City to the Cayo District.

In some areas the vegetation of the river banks is well conserved.

One major river drains the northern slopes of the Maya Mountains. This is the Sibun River, which flows towards the sea south of Belize City. The Sibun River's floods provide water for the lagoons along the coast. These lagoons are Northern Lagoon, Manatee Lagoon, Fabers Lagoon and Jones Lagoon. The Burden Canal links all of these lagoons. These lagoons are home to a great variety of wildlife, some of which is very delicate and near extinction, such as the manatee, the green turtle and the iguana.

The rivers flowing from the eastern slopes of the Maya Mountains pass through the central coastal plains in relatively short and straight courses. They form very fertile lands which are used for agriculture. Most of our banana, citrus and other fruit plantations are found in these areas. These rivers are Mullins River, North Stann Creek River, Sittee River, South Stann Creek River and the Monkey River which, because of a very heavy rainfall, carries as much water as the Belize River.

In the Southern lowlands, the main rivers are the Moho, the Sarstoon and the Temash rivers, whose sources are in Guatemala. They are in the most undeveloped and inaccessible areas of the country. Whenever rivers flow across national borders, political cooperation is essential for their management.

✎ *Draw a map and trace Belize's major rivers. Make a list of towns and villages along these rivers.*

✎ *Trace the course of the Sibun River and the lagoons which it feeds.*

The middle region of the Belize River Valley.

All over Belize small streams serve as an important source of potable water for some small rural communities.

Using Rivers

The Belize River is the main source of water for Belize City, Belmopan, and the villages along its banks. San Ignacio gets its water from the Macal and Dangriga gets water from the North Stann Creek River. Towns in the Toledo District and also in the northern plains get their water from underground **aquifers**.

Pollution and contamination of water is not yet a serious problem in Belize. But waste from toilets that enters rivers can spread serious diseases. Wastes from hospitals, sugar factories and agriculture can make the water unsafe to drink. When waste runs into areas with limestone rocks and seeps underground, springs and wells may become polluted.

Sometimes pollution is not only unsafe, but unpleasant to look at. People may throw trash in the rivers because the current carries it away. But the trash always ends up somewhere.

Rivers have another important use. The fast-flowing currents of some rivers can be dammed and used to produce electric power, called hydroelectricity. The water turns turbines in machines that produce electric currents. This way of making electricity is much cleaner than a power plant driven by gas or diesel motors. But care must be taken about where dams are built. Dams make the rivers behind them swell into small lakes, or reservoirs. It is important not to flood areas that are important for agriculture, ecology, archaeology or settlement. Dams also control major flooding and regulate water flows downstream.

Belize has recently built a hydroelectric dam, the Mollejon Hydro Project. It is located in the Vaca Falls area in the Cayo District, on the Macal River. The goal is to have the dam produce electricity for towns and villages from Benque Viejo to Belize. Eventually the dam may provide electricity for the rest of the country as well.

The Mopan River by the village of San Jose Succotz.

Research and make a list of examples of international cooperation in relation to the use of rivers by two countries.

Observe a river near your locality. Write an essay telling about the misuse and contamination of rivers.

Find out more about the Mollejón Hydro Project and its benefits.

For many years, shallow wells were the only source of water for most villages.

✐ Collect information about water wells in your locality. Find out about their depth, water flow, how long they have been in use, if they are contaminated etc.

Underground water

Although Belize has an abundance of rivers and streams, underneath the ground there is another system of waterways. Layers of rock, gravel and sand beneath the earth trap water. We have previously studied how groundwater is a precious resource in the world.

Underground rivers exist in the karst areas of Belize. Scientists are studying these rivers and finding out how they relate to the water resources of Belize.

Because Belize has so many limestone regions, water empties into these areas easily. Somctimes the water reappears as a spring.

Sometimes wells are dug to reach the water. These wells and springs are used for water supplies throughout the country. Each district has one or more potential aquifers, and small villages have at least one well. Most towns get their water from a town well. Benque Viejo, for instance, is supplied with water from a spring.

Groundwater is usually cleaner than surface water. This is because the rocks and soils through which it runs help to filter out harmful substances.

The Sibun River emerges from a cave.

Chapter 10
Climate and Weather

In our study of the geography of Belize, we have seen the links between different aspects of our land. Geology has affected soil; soil has affected our land use. Now we will take a look at another influence on our land and our lives: the climate and weather of Belize. Climate, you will recall, is the state of the atmosphere over a long period of time. Weather is the day to day condition of the elements: temperature, humidity, rainfall, wind direction and speed, clouds and sunshine.

The climate and weather in Belize affect our daily lives. But the climate also has an effect on many aspects of geography, and directly or indirectly influences every human activity.

Year round swimming is possible in the warm waters of the Caribbean Sea.

Climate and its Influences

Belize is located at 15 to 19 degrees latitude north of the equator. This puts us in the subtropics. Subtropical regions have special characteristics in climate that distinguish them from other regions. The change of seasons is measured by the presence or absence of rainfall as well as changes in temperatures. The closer to the equator a country is located, the more important rainfall patterns become. In temperate regions, cold winters and warm summers mark the seasons.

How does Belize's climate affect agriculture? How does it affect different aspects of our lives?

Our location near the tropics determines our climate and influences our lifestyles.

Meteorological instruments provide data on weather conditions.

An anemometre, an instrument used to measure wind speed.

✐✐Make a time line showing the main seasons in Belize and their main characteristics.

In Belize, latitude is the main influence on the climate. There are other things that influence climate too. For instance, the distance of a place from the sea or its height above sea level, both affect its temperature. Wind is air in motion and it also affects temperature and rainfall. It may come from a warm or a cold region, and it may blow from the direction of the sea or the land. Some winds blow constantly, like Trade Winds, while others vary in intensity from weak to strong. Belize gets the benefits of the Trade Winds which generally blow from the east around 16 kilometres an hour.

The seasons in Belize

There are two major seasons: the wet and the dry season, and there is also a season of northerlies.

The wet season extends from June to November. This is caused by tropical systems such as tropical waves, tropical storms and hurricanes.

The dry season is from March to June. It is caused by the effect of the Bermuda-Azores high pressure system over our region.

The Northers

Northers are cold, relatively wet air masses that flow from the north. These winds are often pushed far by air masses in the Arctic during the months of October to April. They bring cool temperatures, heavy rains and choppy seas. However from February to April they are much dryer but can produce severe thunderstorms.

A norther in San Pedro, Ambergris Caye.

Temperature: Tropical Heat

Temperature is a measure of warmth and coolness. Temperature is measured by thermometers, which show the amount of heat in the air. Temperature can be measured by degrees Celsius or Fahrenheit.

By using thermometers, we can record temperature changes throughout the day and over the years. When meteorologists record temperatures for a long period of time, they can calculate a region's mean annual temperature. Belize's mean annual temperature varies from 26°C, or 78°F, along the coast to 21°C, or 63°F, in the upper reaches of the Maya Mountains.

The hottest temperature ever recorded in Belize was in May 1976 in Belmopan when the temperature reached 43°C, or 110°F. The lowest was in December 1968 at Sibun Hill, Cayo District with a temperature of 4°C, or 40°F.

In Belize, the sea affects the temperature. Cool breezes blow from sea to land during the day, and cool the hot air over the land. As we go further away from the coast, this effect weakens. San Ignacio, for instance, is not affected by sea breezes. At the end of the dry season from April to May, the midday temperatures may often be over 38C°, or 100°F .

Altitude, the height of the land above the sea, also affects the temperature. For each 160 metres we climb, the temperature falls by 1°C (3 to 5°F for every 1,000 feet). The temperature in the Maya Mountains, therefore, is usually lower than on the plains. Here the wind also blows stronger, and helps to lower temperatures.

Humidity

Humidity is a measure of the water vapour in the air. The heat we feel during the day can also be influenced by humidity. Measurements of humidity are made in percentages. The relative humidity is a percentage of the total moisture that the air can hold.

Warm air can hold more moisture than cooler air. In Belize the humidity is often very high. The air in the Trade Winds

A rain-water vat.

What is the difference between Celsius and Fahrenheit?

Record the temperature once a week for a month in both Celsius and Fahrenheit.

Find out the annual mean temperature in your district.

Nimbus clouds usually bring rain.

passes over the moist Caribbean Sea. This causes the coastal areas to be more humid than the inland areas of Belize. Humidity, like temperature, changes during the day and between seasons.

Rainfall

Our life depends on rainfall. It allows crops and the forests to grow properly and gives us clean, safe water. Too little rain can harm the land. But too much rainfall can damage or destroy crops, roads and bridges.

Throughout Belize there is a wet and dry season. In the north, the dry season may last 3 to 4 months from February to May. In the south, the dry season may be as short as a few weeks. San Ignacio receives 114 days of rain in a year. In Punta Gorda, the amount increases to 166 days. A month is dry when less than 100 milimetres, or 4 inches, of rainfall occurs in that period.

Mountains and hills influence rainfall. They force warm and very humid air to rise quickly. When the wind blows clouds in from the Caribbean Sea, these clouds rise above the mountains and the moisture condenses to cause rainfall.

For this reason, the southern region of the Maya Mountains receives the most rainfall in Belize. On the south-eastern side of the mountains, the land elevation changes quickly. By the time rain clouds cross over to the western side, they have lost

Conduct an experiment to measure rainfall.

Look at the diagram in the atlas. Explain how the Maya Mountains influence rainfall in the country.

Explain how rainfall affects agriculture and vegetation.

Find out the average annual rainfall in your locality or district.

The swollen waters of the Mopan River.

After weeks without rain, clay soils become dry and cracked.

A fire lookout.

most of their moisture. This effect is called a rain shadow. This influence of the Maya Mountains affects the rainfall pattern of the entire country.

Rainfall affects agriculture and vegetation in Belize. The lower amount of rain in the north is good for sugar cane. In the south the high temperatures and rainfall are good for bananas, cocoa and citrus.

Milpa farmers depend on the rainfall for their planting schedule. In the north, limestone areas can become very dry without rain. The long wet season in the south also produces our lush rain forests.

Talk to a farmer and find out how, throughout the year, weather influences agricultural activities.

Weather Hazards: Floods, Droughts and Storms

A drought occurs when very little rain is received during the year. This affects plant and animal life as well as people. With little available moisture trees can die and crops can be damaged. Another hazard which occurs during the dry season comes from lightning. Lightning can start a fire. Pine trees and dry grasses burn quickly, especially when fanned by strong winds. The Forest Department of Belize watches for these fires in tall towers called look-outs. If they see smoke or fire, a fire-fighting team rushes to the area, travelling on roads built specifically for this purpose.

A lot of rain or a severe storm can cause floods. This is not so much a danger in the north, where much of the rainwater goes

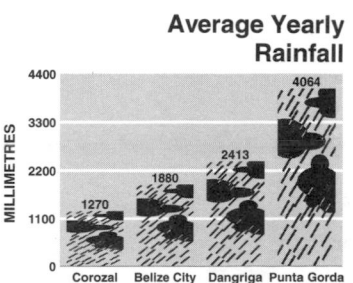

Average Yearly Rainfall

MILLIMETRES

Corozal	Belize City	Dangriga	Punta Gorda
1270	1880	2413	4064

Corozal Town gets only one-third of the rain of Punta Gorda.

The Macal River often floods the town of San Ignacio in the rainy season.

into the limestone underground. But in the mountains, the water runs down the slopes into surface streams and rivers. When it reaches the plains below, the rivers rise rapidly. Rivers may swell to as much as 6 to 9 metres higher than normal causing destruction to property, roads, bridges and crops.

Both droughts and floods affect our drinking water. During the dry season, there is often a shortage of available water. People often collect rainwater during the wet season in vats and barrels. When there is a lot of water, the rivers become brown and dirty from the silt and sediment that washes down.

Although Belize's location in the subtropics gives it enjoyable warm weather, the same location brings dangerous weather systems. These two patterns are northers and hurricanes.

Hurricanes are dangerous. Hurricanes are low pressure systems that cover very large areas. They develop over tropical seas and bring high winds and extreme rainfall to Belize.

Find out about the biggest floods that have affected your area in the past 5 years.

Find out about major hurricanes that have struck Belize since 1930 and how they affected Belize's landscape.

Depending on wind speed and how long they last, storms are classified into different types. If the winds are less than 62 kilometres an hour, is called a tropical depression. Higher winds between 63 and 117 kilometres an hour are called tropical storms. A storm is called a hurricane when its winds reach speeds of over 118 kilometres an hour.

The aftermath of Hurricane Hattie, 1961.

Hurricanes in Belize

A hurricane is a large mass of air spinning at high speed. In this mass, wind moves to the centre of the storm, or the eye. As it reaches the eye, the wind moves faster and faster. Around the eye of the hurricane, the wind shoots upward like smoke in a chimney. Inside the eye there is no wind. The eye of a hurricane can be several kilometres in diameter.

Hurricanes are so destructive because the storm surge, or high tide ahead of the storm, can be very high. They batter and flood coastal areas. High winds may cause damage to buildings, agricultural crops and forests. Hurricanes can also destroy coral reefs, and shift beaches and sand bars kilometres. The most vulnerable lands are small narrow cayes with little vegetation. Large amounts of rain may flood areas further inland from the coast.

The hurricane season extends from June to November. The majority of hurricanes in Belize occur in September.

Weather Forecasting: Being Prepared

Because of the danger of hurricanes and other weather systems, the work of people who watch how weather develops is very important. These people are called meteorologists. In Belize, the National Meteorological Service, aided by modern technology, receives satellite images and weather data from around the world. This information, along with local data from stations around Belize, is processed and used to develop weather forecasts.

Advisories and warnings of approaching storms are broadcast on local radio and TV stations. The Hydrology Service also advises on floods and droughts.

We may not be able to change the weather, but thanks to meteorologists we can at least be prepared.

A satellite image of the eye of a hurricane.

In 1961 Hurricane Hattie split Caye Caulker in two.

✎ *Write a short composition about the government's hurricane plan, including its main purposes before and after a hurricane strikes.*

✎✎ *Make a list of important things to do in preparation for a hurricane.*

Chapter 11
Our Environment

Until 150 years ago, prior to the industrial revolution, the Earth's waters were unpolluted, the air was clean and large tracts of undisturbed forest were the home of millions of plant, animal and insect species.

Unfortunately all this has changed. Today, factories pollute our land and water. Millions of motor vehicles send harmful gases into the atmosphere. Tons of garbage are produced every day and have to be disposed of.

The world's population is increasing at a rate of about 2 per cent every year. Forests are being cut down to make room for housing developments and to grow more food. Much of the Earth's forests are quickly disappearing.

Along with the forests, countless animal and plant species are also disappearing due to the loss of their habitats. In the past 100 years many plant and animal species have become extinct. Once an animal or plant is extinct it is gone forever from the Earth's surface.

The Biosphere

The living world as a whole is known as the **biosphere**. Every part of the biosphere interacts with each other. The biosphere is so

Explain the main causes for the degradation of the environment in the past 150 years.

Explain the meaning and significance of extinction.

Name some of the endangered species of Belize. Find out the reason why they are in danger.

Untouched landscape.

Deforestation has serious consequences.

complex that global interactions are difficult to study. To study the living world we divide it into smaller units called ecosystems.

An ecosystem is a biological community of interacting organisms and their physical environment. Each ecosystem has its own system for creating and sustaining life. Each life form is dependent on others for food, protection or shelter. When one link in this chain of life is destroyed, everything else in this ecosystem is affected. Belize, though a very small country, has five major ecosystems: tropical **rainforest**, mangroves, savannas, wetlands and coral reefs.

Ecology is the study of the complex interactions within ecosystems. For example, an ecologist may study the effects of different plants on the kinds of birds found in a community, or the effects of the introduction of an exotic species of fish, plant or animal on the local species.

Our Natural Environment

Our natural **environment** harbours an incredible range of plant and animal species. Belize has at least 4,000 species of native flowering plants, 250 kinds of orchids, and 700 native trees. Our plants and trees are researched by international organizations looking for new cures to diseases.

With its abundant forests, Belize provides a relatively safe environment for many animals. There are more than 150 species of mammals, including 70 species of bats, as well as howler monkeys, brocket deer, otters, jaguars, ocelots, margays, jaguarundis, pumas and tapirs. In many other tropical countries these animals are endangered or extinct. Many of the animals found in Belize depend on the conservation of the forests.

Birds are also abundant. There are approximately 520 species, including ducks, kites, kingfishers, jabiru storks, frigatebirds, hawks, eagles, spoonbills, vultures, hummingbirds, owls, toucans, nine different parrot species and one species of macaw. Of this number, 370 are permanent residents of Belize.

Hunting and illegal trading in pets and wild animal hides can harm animal populations. Sometimes smugglers try to take parrots, macaws, toucans, snakes and lizards out of the country to

Our forests are a rich source of useful plants.

Give examples of a marine and a forest community and illustrate them.

Observe and write a description of the birds you see. Find out their names and habitats.

A reef ecosystem.

Jaguars are protected in Belize.

✐ Make a list of coastal settlements and locate them on a map.

✐✐ Name a few communities which are close to the reef. Find out the many benefits of living close to the reef.

✐ Make a drawing of a marine ecosystem.

sell as pets. Crocodile skins and jaguar hides are sought after but they are illegal to take out of the country or even to have. The Forest Department and Customs Department both enforce these laws to make sure our natural heritage is protected.

Belize has a rich diversity of coastal and marine ecosystems. Coastal lagoons near the shore and mangroves provide many nutrients that flow into the sea. Both also serve as nurseries and feeding grounds for many fish species. Coral reefs and tropical rainforests are some of the Earth's richest biological communities. Belize's Barrier Reef provides a home for a wide variety of life and, like mangroves, protects the coast from stormy seas.

Marine animals like dolphins, salt-water crocodiles, manatees and sea turtles do well in the sparsely populated areas of the coast and cayes.

The income of many people relies on the health of the coast. Approximately 40 per cent of the population resides along the coast or on the cayes. The country's major industries, tourism and fishing, also depend on a healthy coastal environment.

Protected Areas

These are specially designated areas set aside to protect the natural environment. Many countries are now trying to protect their environments by declaring certain land, sea or coastal areas as protected areas. Protected areas are the home of many species of birds, fish and plants. Belize has set aside large areas of land protecting more than 120 species of mammals of which nine are endangered or threatened with extinction.

But declaring an area protected does not necessarily mean it will not be damaged. Due to a shortage of money and workers to enforce the law, people who do not care about the protection of the environment continue to plunder and destroy our natural treasures. For example, some small mangrove cayes that were declared bird sanctuaries in the 1970s have since been destroyed by hunters and fishermen.

Guanacaste Park, Cayo District.

The ancient milpa system of the Maya allows the vegetation to re-grow.

How People Change the Environment

Early settlers in Belize were attracted by its rich forests. Logging was selective and most of the forests were spared. When forest products became less profitable people turned to agriculture. As Belize's population increases and we try to grow more of our own food, pressure for more cleared land will grow. People can farm without causing too much damage to the environment by using healthy and sustainable agricultural practices such as organic farming or agroforestry.

Deforestation

The temporary or permanent clearing of forests for agriculture or other purposes is called deforestation. Forests in Belize are cleared for "slash and burn" subsistence, or milpa farming, and for one-crop agriculture such as citrus. There are two types of forest clearing: selective and clear-cutting. In selective logging trees of a specific size and species are cut while the surrounding forest is left intact. Selective logging can cause a lot of damage if not carried out with adequate pre-planning to avoid damage to the surrounding forest.

Clear-cutting is the removal of all trees in a selected area. The forest is totally cut with a great loss of **biodiversity**. In both cases reforestation, or the planting of the trees to restore the forest, is very important.

Locate protected areas in your atlas. Find out about newly established areas. Find out the reasons for their establishment.

Describe the negative effects of deforestation.

Find out the meanings of "organic farming" and "agroforestry".

Vegetation protects river banks from erosion.

Erosion

Erosion, the wearing away of soil by wind and water, is a serious and dangerous result of deforestation. Trees in a forest act as a big sponge, absorbing rainfall and controlling the water that flows into river systems. When trees are cut down there are no roots to hold the soil in place and it washes away with the rains. Leaving a strip of forested land between clearings and a belt of trees along rivers and other waterways helps to prevent soil erosion and river sedimentation.

Clearing hillsides for planting causes erosion of topsoil. Rain carries away the top soil leaving the slopes barren. The soil is washed into rivers as silt and eventually reaches the sea where it can damage our reefs by smothering the coral polyps. By blocking the sunlight it also kills algae that live inside the polyps.

Erosion of topsoil is a major cause of declines in agricultural productivity since many soil nutrients are found in top soil.

Polluting Our Land, Air and Water

What are the major causes of pollution in Belize?

Can you think of any ways in which pollution can be reduced in Belize? What can you do personally?

Observe and describe the different causes of water, land and air pollution in Belize.

All of us are responsible for the use and management of our environment. Pollution means spoiling or harming the environment by emission of waste products. While some pollution is due to natural causes, most pollution is caused by people.

Solid waste pollutes land, water and air. The increasing amount of garbage generated by people has led to the increase of garbage which is periodically burned or used as landfill.

Open air garbage dump.

When garbage is burned, toxic fumes pollute the air. Garbage dumps become breeding grounds for disease-carrying animals. Much of what is considered garbage can be recycled.

Garbage thrown into streams pollutes the water and affects people living downstream. Eventually it may find its way to the sea. Plastics are especially harmful as plastic bags float, resembling jellyfish which sea turtles like to eat. Turtles ingest the plastics which soon suffocates them. Waterfowl can be strangled by fishing lines.

Some industrial wastes dumped into the sea or into rivers are extremely toxic and can kill and contaminate fish species. Eating contaminated fish can cause illness in humans. Sewage emptied into rivers and streams contaminate drinking water and can cause serious health problems such as cholera.

Agro-industries are the largest producers of waste in Belize. Liquid waste from citrus and sugar factories runs into rivers and harms plant and animal life. The citrus industry often dumps fermented pulp into rivers.

Farmers in Belize often use chemicals to fertilize land or rid it of pests. But the misuse of chemicals has led to many problems. People who spread the chemicals are sometimes made ill by them and the crops they harvest can contain harmful chemical residues. These chemicals can also seep into the ground and pollute both the soil and underground water.

Things We Can Do to Save the Earth

Today's new technologies use the sun and wind to generate power. Much of the garbage we produce can be recycled, some at home, some in factories. We can recycle paper, aluminum, glass, old clothes and plastic. Organic matter such as vegetable peels, food scraps, grass clippings, sawdust and cow manure can in a short time be changed into rich black soil to be spread on fields as fertilizer. This process is called composting.

Belize's low population and small number of industries are the main reasons we still have a relatively healthy environment. However, this should only make us more aware of the problems we may create as our population grows and development follows its course.

Chapter 12
The People of Belize

Compared to most other countries, Belize has a small population. The latest census showed that over 240,204 people live in Belize in an area of 22,962 square kilometers or 8,866 square miles of land. With so few people living in a large amount of land, Belize's population density is low. There are only 10.5 people per square kilometer, in contrast with El Salvador, which has 301. In this chapter we will study the make up and some of the social characteristics of our population.

Belize's last population census was in 2000. A census collects information about a country's population. This data is used mainly by government agencies but also by businesses. It is important to see how population has changed over time to help in planning for employment, for schools and teachers, and for services such as water, power and garbage collection. In the past 100 years, Belize's population has grown quickly because of increased births and immigration.

Belize's recent history is one of immigration, and we have welcomed people who, for one reason or another, left their homeland. Our country offers all its citizens a peaceful existence with full respect for their human rights and for each ethnic group's history and culture. Many of us do not identify our-

Name some of the information collected in a census.

Compare the figures from the last two censuses for your community. What do the figures tell you?

What are the main causes for emigration and immigration? Interview an immigrant family and find out why they decided to migrate.

Belize's multiethnic society: learning from our differences.

selves with just one group. For example, if my mother is Mestizo and my father Creole, I may identify with one or both groups. But above all, we are all Belizeans enjoying the same rights and appreciating our unique blend of traditions and heritage. All ethnic groups without exception have contributed enormously to the creation of a Belizean culture and to Belize's development.

Population Density and Distribution

In cities, the population density is higher than in rural areas. In order of size, the eight largest settlements are Belize City, Orange Walk, San Ignacio/Santa Elena, Dangriga, Corozal, Benque Viejo del Carmen, Belmopan and Punta Gorda. In most countries, more and more people move from rural areas to urban centres, but in Belize, the rural and urban populations are about equal. Outside of the towns, most people live in small villages along rivers and main roads and along the coast or cayes. Elsewhere, much of Belize is still thinly populated.

Both young and old play an important role in Belizean society.

Social Characteristics

Populations can be described by important social characteristics. Age, sex, health, education, language, religion and ethnicity define who we are. We can study these characteristics to see how things have changed over time, and how they differ from region to region. The most unique feature of Belize's population is its variety of people.

What are the two reasons for population growth?

Find out some of the reasons for the location of Belize's largest settlements.

Belize has a young population. Our high birthrate and low death rate means that today, about 42 per cent of our population is under 15 years old. Improved health conditions have resulted in people now living longer, and the percentage of people aged 65 years and older is increasing. Large populations of young and old people mean that more of the country's resources have to be spent on services like education and health. It also means the number of people who can work is relatively small. The ratio of men to women changes frequently, but today there are more men than women. Proper nutrition, good housing, a safe supply of water and a clean environment improve the health of a community. Other factors like education, rewarding and satisfying jobs, recreation and sports, and a healthy social environment are all important for good health.

Based on a survey of your town or neighborhood, find the reasons why people migrate from rural to urban areas more often?

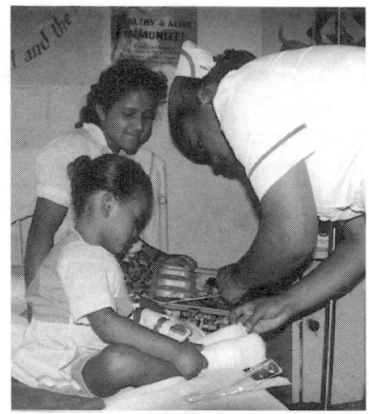

Free immunizations are available at hospitals and village clinics throughout Belize.

Belize City still stands as the largest and oldest settlement in Belize.

Students can borrow books from libraries for research or for the pleasure of reading.

✎✎ *List traffic safety rules that are important for children to know. In groups, make a poster illustrating each rule and display them at your school.*

✎ *Find out what the main causes of traffic accidents are in your area and how they could have been prevented.*

Overall, 90 per cent of children in Belize have been immunized against the most dangerous childhood diseases. The spread of AIDS is a very serious problem in Belize and the Caribbean, and the infection rate is now second only to sub-Saharan Africa. Every year, more and more people die or are injured in traffic accidents.

Schools in Belize are classified into four levels: pre-school, primary, secondary and tertiary education. Primary education in Belize is free and compulsory for children from age five to fourteen. Literacy, or the ability to read and write, is an important indicator in any society. Of Belize's population over 14 years old, 70.3 are literate and 19.8 are semi-literate.

Education is a basic human need and human right. It enables people to gain the knowledge and skills they need for effective participation in society. Education is obtained in schools and also by informal means such as the mass media or by reading and work experience. These two forms of learning are both important.

Language, Religion and Ethnicity

Because of Belize's diverse population, many people speak more than one language. More than half of our population speaks English or Creole and 44 per cent speaks Spanish. A variety of other languages such as Maya, Garifuna and German are also spoken. It is important that languages are not lost or forgotten. Over 62 per cent of our people speak two or more languages. Knowing many languages helps us to communicate with people from other cultures and nationalities.

Belizeans practice many different religions. Nearly two-thirds of our population is Roman Catholic, and the rest include Protestant, Anglican, Methodist, Baptist, Seventh Day Adventist, Bahai, Mormon and Mennonite, among others. The various ethnic groups have traditional religious beliefs although many have also adopted the religions just mentioned.

A group of people who share a common religion, customs, music, language and racial characteristics is called an ethnic group. Belize's many ethnic groups have helped to create a rich and distinct Belizean identity, where each culture contributes to the Belizean character.

Benque Viejo's Catholic church was built in1941.

The Maya

The Maya were the first inhabitants of Belize. Their civilization flourished in the area from 900 BC to 900 AD, after which their population of one million sharply declined. Today the Maya of Belize make up approximately 11 per cent of the population, and come from several distinct groups.

The Yucatec Maya fiercely resisted Spanish attempts to conquer their land. Still, many were forced to flee south from the Yucatan in the 15th century and again during the Caste War of the 1840s, along with Mestizos, to settle in Corozal and Orange Walk Districts. There they turned from their subsistence agriculture to sugar cane production. The Mopan Maya migrated from Peten, Guatemala in the 1880s because of oppression, forced labour and military recruitment, lack of land, low wages, and persecution. In 1884 the K'ekchi' Maya left Alta Vera Paz, Guatemala and settled in villages in the Toledo District.

Most Maya are dedicated to subsistence agriculture, but recently some Maya villages in the Toledo District have begun to benefit from eco-tourism through Maya guesthouses and the sale of handicrafts such as baskets and embroidery.

The Maya of Belize are proud of their culture and history and have retained their language, music, dance, food and customs,

Take a census in your class and make a chart showing how many boys, girls, ethnic groups and languages are represented. Calculate the percentages.

In your words, define what an ethnic group is. Give some examples.

Make up a chart showing some characteristics of Belize's ethnic groups.

83

Maya harp player.

often holding their traditional beliefs alongside Christian ones. The K'ekchi' have remained the most traditional group. They continue to practice the ancient rituals and hold the belief that land is to be shared among the community. In 1978, they formed the Maya Cultural Council, which manages land reserves in the Toledo District granted to them by the Government.

Maize has always been the staple of the Maya diet. It is used in tortillas, tamales and porridge, and eaten with beans, chilies, squash, game meat, chicken and pork. In ancient times, a spicy chocolate mix was the favourite drink of the upper classes of Maya society, and cacao beans were used as a form of money. They could truly say that money grew on trees.

Maya celebrations include music played on the chirimia, a double reed flute and drums. Harp, guitar, violins and marimba are added according to the occasion. Many dances are still performed, including the famous Deer Dance ceremony, which is enacted over a nine-day period.

Make a timeline that shows the Maya presence in Belize from ancient times to the more recent migrations.

Try making some corn tortillas for your family or any other food from one of Belize's groups.

The Mestizo

The Mestizos are of Spanish and Maya descent. In the 1840's, thousands of Mestizo refugees fled from the Caste War of Yucatan, Mexico, and settled in the northern part of Belize, mainly in the Corozal and Orange Walk areas, Ambergris Caye and Caye Caulker. Some settled in Cayo.

Mestizo dancers entertain visitors at the annual El Pilar fiesta.

Belize's bright future shows in the faces of these Creole students.

Mr. Peters and his Boom and Chime band have entertained generations of Belizeans with their traditional Creole music.

At about the same time another migration of Mestizos was taking place in Western Belize. Guatemala had obtained its independence from Spain and many Mestizos from Peten were fleeing from a dictatorial regime, and settling mainly in San Ignacio and Benque Viejo del Carmen.

Regardless of their origin, the Mestizos in Belize are a homogeneous group, which means that they all share the same ethnic and cultural characteristics. They speak Spanish and the majority belongs to the Catholic religion. Many are involved in agriculture, fishing, and business.

The Mestizo culture consists of a combination of Spanish and Maya customs and beliefs. Some believe in supernatural beings such as "El Duende", "La Llorona" and ghosts. The spirits of the dead are honoured by traditional offerings on All Saints Day and All Souls Day.

The diet of the Mestizos consists of dishes that reflect Spanish and Maya influences. Some examples of these are: tamalitos, bollos, escabeche and relleno (Spanish); beans, tortillas, and chile (Maya). The Mestizos have traditional dances such as the "Toro" dance and the "Mestizada". The guitar and the marimba accompany these dances.

The Creole

In Belize, the term Creole is defined as a person of both European and African ancestry. As the British Baymen of the 1700s mixed with their African slaves, the combined influences formed the Creole culture. The slaves came from different parts

In groups, find out about the different religions practised in Belize. In which ways are they similar and in which ways are they different?

Tell stories of "El Duende" and "La Llorona". In groups, write and illustrate these stories.

85

Music and dance are an enjoyable part of life for Garifuna children.

of Africa and were forced to speak English to communicate with one another. However, they altered the English words to create a language of their own which allowed them to pass on African values and wisdom. Proverbs and the stories of Anansi the Spider, Bra Tiger and other animals are still heard today. Burial practices such as wakes follow African traditions, as do practices of witchcraft or obeah. Almost all people of Belize speak Creole today and until recently they were the largest ethnic group.

Singing and dancing were two ways in which the African slaves expressed themselves, and the drum was their most important musical instrument. Today popular Creole music styles include "Brukdown" and "Boom and Chime", which use gourd rattles, scrapers, guitars, and the jawbone of a donkey or cow for percussion. Drummers in Gales Point Manatee are reviving the traditional music and drum making craft of their African ancestors.

The diet of the Creole also has African roots. It consists of ground foods, such as cassava, yam and sweet potato, which are combined with other European dishes. Belize's national dish of rice and beans, made with coconut oil or coconut milk, is typical of Creole cooking.

The Garifuna

The Garifuna people are the descendants of a group of African slaves who were shipwrecked on the island of St. Vincent in the seventeenth century and inter-married with the Arawak Indians who lived there. In 1795, five thousand Garifuna were forcefully deported from their homeland and brought to Honduras. In 1902 approximately 150 Garifuna settled in Belize. Today, they are found in Belize, Guatemala, and Honduras. In Belize, the main Garifuna towns are Dangriga, Hopkins, Seine Bight, Georgetown, Punta Gorda, and Barranco. They speak the Garifuna language, and retain their African beliefs and customs combined with Christian influences. These include rites to communicate with their ancestors , which are performed to resolve personal, financial and health problems. These rites help strengthen the ties among friends and relatives in the community and help to preserve the culture.

✎ Collect Creole proverbs. Illustrate them and add a glossary of Creole words and their English meaning. Bind them into a book and present them to your school library.

✎ Divide into groups. Choose a period of Garifuna history and reenact each one.

86

The Garifuna are very creative people. Among them we find painters, drummers, singers, dancers, and composers, teachers and other professionals. Their most popular dance, the "Punta", is now danced throughout Belize.

The Garifuna diet consists mainly of fish, meat, plantain, cassava, coconut and other ground foods. Traditionally, men are fishermen while the women are farmers. Today, the Garifuna make up five per cent of the population of Belize.

The many faces of Belize

The East Indians

In the 1850's, indentured servants were brought to Belize from India to work on the sugar plantations of Corozal and Toledo Districts. They were known as "Coolies", which meant paid servant. After their five-year contracts expired they settled in places like Calcutta and Estrella in the Corozal District, and Forest Home and Fairview in the Toledo District. Some of their traditions are still preserved.

In the 20th century more Indian citizens established themselves as business people in Belize City and other major towns. Many of the new immigrants still practice their culture and religion, and speak their languages. The descendants of the East Indians and the new arrivals today make up two per cent of the population of Belize.

Make a chart listing the words for "Hello", "Goodbye", "Thank you" and "Friend" in English, Creole, Spanish, Maya, Garifuna, German, Chinese, Indian and Lebanese languages.

Rice is the staple food of the Chinese and is commonly eaten with chopsticks.

A young Mennonite girl dressed in traditional costume.

How did the immigration of Mennonites affect Belize's society? Make a list of products your family uses that are produced by Mennonites?

Plan a cultural fair at your school with food, music and dance presentations representing each of Belize's ethnic groups.

The People of the Middle East

Immigrants from Lebanon, Palestine, and Jordan came to Belize around 1870 and settled in Benque Viejo and San Ignacio. They initially worked in the chicle and logging industries, and later established businesses in Cayo and Belize City that their descendants continue today. Some have retained their language and their traditional foods, such as kibi and humus. They place great value on the family and the majority belongs to the Catholic Church.

The Chinese

About two hundred Chinese came to Belize when Japan invaded China in the 1940s. Most settled in the main towns and established businesses while a few continued farming.

Many of the Chinese people in Belize still practice their culture, language, Buddhist religion and celebrations such as the Chinese New Year. In recent times many Chinese from both Taiwan and China have come to Belize and established businesses. Industrious and peace loving, the Chinese make an important contribution to Belizean society.

The Mennonites

The Mennonites are a German-speaking religious group that originated in the sixteenth century in the Netherlands. They have migrated throughout their history in order to follow their beliefs in a simple and pacifist existence. About 3,500 Mennonites came to Belize from Mexico in 1958. The Mennonites in Belize range from very traditional groups that do not allow the use of machinery to modern and liberal groups.

The largest community of the Mennonites is Spanish Lookout. They can also be found in Barton Creek, Blue Creek and Shipyard. Their society is self-governed and is based on their religious beliefs. The Government of Belize does not intervene in their affairs. The majority of Mennonites are modern farmers and have taken advantage of technology to produce milk, cheese, eggs, poultry, and other products. More recently they have moved into logging, furniture, and construction.

Chapter 13
Our System of Government

When Belize became independent on September 21st 1981, it adopted a system of representative parliamentary democracy, patterned after the British Parliament at Westminster. In this system, the Queen remains the head of state of Belize, but leaders chosen by the people conduct the government. These leaders are chosen in elections held at regular intervals.

The Belize flag: a symbol of our national identity.

The Governor-General is the representative of the Queen in Belize and appears on her behalf at national and international functions. The Governor-General must be a Belizean and is responsible for approving the appointment of the Prime Minister and members of the Cabinet and Senate.

All citizens who are eighteen years or older may vote for their representatives at elections held at the national, municipal or village level. During a political campaign candidates from all parties present their views to the public. In a democracy, voters have a responsibility to be informed and to cast their ballot for the person they feel will best represent them.

Find out which other countries have similar systems of government. Why do you think this is so? In groups, find out about other systems of government in the Americas. Present your findings to the class.

The government in power calls elections no later than five years after they have been voted into office. The Elections and Boundaries Commission makes sure the election is fair. Persons who are elected to political office are authorized by our Constitution to govern the country, but they are accountable for their decisions to the people who elected them.

Stage a mock general election for your electoral division. Select a social issue such as crime, environmental degradation, unemployment, youth issues etc. Select standard bearers to contest the election. Prepare campaigns and debates. Finally go to the polls.

Electoral Divisions and Municipalities

Belize is divided into twenty-nine electoral units, known as constituencies. The six districts are divided so each constituency is made up of relatively equal numbers of voters.

A representative is elected in each constituency and becomes a member of the House of Representatives. He or she responds to the interests of the people living in that area. Each district is also divided into smaller areas called municipalities.

In Belize City and Belmopan, the area is governed by a City Council, and in the other districts by Town Councils.

Belize's Governor General.

The National Assembly Building in Belmopan where the House of Representatives and the Senate meet.

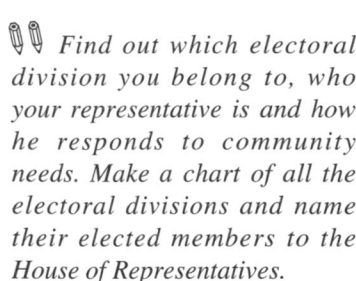

Find out which electoral division you belong to, who your representative is and how he responds to community needs. Make a chart of all the electoral divisions and name their elected members to the House of Representatives.

Find a copy of the Constitution, discuss the rights and responsibilities described there. Write an essay on the topic "the will of the people shall form the basis of government."

Municipalities have power only over the boundaries of the city or the town. In places where there are too few people to form a City Council or a Town Council, Village Councils are created. In some Maya communities, the traditional alcalde system is used. An alcalde or village leader is elected every year to lead the village.

The Constitution of Belize, which is the highest law of the land, describes how the country is governed. It protects the principles of human rights and freedoms and states that all citizens are to be treated equally under the law regardless of their race, colour, creed or sex. Children are protected equally whatever their economic or social status, and the government must provide for their education and health care.

The Constitution requires that government policies "protect the rights of the individual to life, liberty and the pursuit of happiness." It guarantees each citizen the right to own land, run a business, work and have access to social security. The Constitution states that "the will of the people shall form the basis of government."

There are three branches of Government: the Executive, the Legislative, and the Judiciary.

The Executive Branch

The Executive Branch has authority through a Cabinet of Ministers headed by the Prime Minister. The function of the

Executive is to make and implement policies and programmes for the benefit of the country. To do this, the Executive relies on the advice and knowledge of the administration, a group of professional civil servants appointed by an independent Public Services Commission.

The Prime Minister, who is appointed by the Governor-General, must be a member of the House of Representatives and the leader of the political party that won the most seats. If no party wins a clear majority, the Governor-General chooses a member of the House who is capable of understanding and representing the needs of the people and fulfilling the demanding requirements of the job. The Prime Minister is responsible for leading the country, setting policies through the Cabinet and aiding communication and coordination between ministries. He or she must also represent Belize to the rest of the world as its head of state. The Prime Minister negotiates with other governments and participates in international organizations and alliances.

The Cabinet is responsible for making policies. Members are chosen from the National Assembly by the Prime Minister. The list of names is submitted to the Governor-General who makes the final appointment. Each member of Cabinet is assigned a Ministry and is responsible for its interests.. The number of ministers is not set and may change with the needs of the country.

Minister of Human Development Women and Civil Society Hon. Dolores Balderamos Garcia.

Divide into groups. Assign a Ministry to each group. Find out what problems each Ministry needs to address. Stage a Cabinet Meeting with a representative of each group and present to the class.

The Cabinet of Ministers.

The Prime Minister of Belize Hon. Said Musa.

The Prime Minister or another minister he appoints in his absence chairs cabinet meetings. Cabinet members may discuss and even disagree on issues brought up at the meetings, but once a vote is taken the decision is final. If a minister is strongly against a policy decision, then he or she may offer to resign from the Cabinet or be asked to do so by the Prime Minister. Cabinet discussions, agreements and documents are kept confidential unless the Cabinet chooses to make them public.

The Legislative Branch

The Legislative Branch is called the National Assembly. It is made up of two Houses, the House of Representatives and the Senate. The National Assembly debates and enacts laws to promote and protect the interests and rights of citizens.

The House of Representatives is made up of the representatives elected from the twenty-nine constituencies of the country. The political party that gains the largest number of seats in the House of Representatives forms the Government; the party with the next highest number of seats forms the Opposition. The leader of the party that forms the Government is appointed Prime Minister. The leader of the largest opposition group is called the Leader of the Opposition. A Speaker presides over the meetings of the House of Representatives.

The Senate is a body of twelve prominent persons who are appointed by the Governor General on the advice of the Prime Minister, the Leader of the Opposition and Civil Society organizations. This body reviews the laws passed by the House of Representatives and ratifies them. They can delay laws passed by the House of Representatives, but cannot reject them. The Senate also ratifies treaties signed by the Government, and approves the appointment of sensitive senior posts, like those of Judges, Ambassadors, and the Auditor General.

The Judiciary

The third branch of Government is the Judiciary. This consists of a Supreme Court of Judicature and a Court of Appeal.

Make a diagram that shows how a law is proposed, debated, amended and ratified.

Organise a sitting of the House of Representatives in your classroom to present, debate and vote on a new law that is important to children.

Supreme Court judges in session.

The Supreme Court is the highest court in the country and can hear and determine any civil or criminal proceedings under any law. The Court of Appeal is a superior court of record and has the jurisdiction and power to hear and determine appeals in civil and criminal matters. The Supreme Court is headed by the Chief Justice, assisted by other judges as required. The Chief Justice is appointed by the Governor-General acting on the advice of the Prime Minister and the Leader of the Opposition with the consent of the Senate. There are also lesser Courts, known as Magistrate's Courts, which hear civil and criminal cases. These Courts may refer cases to the Supreme Court. There is also a Family Court that deals with civil matters of a domestic nature.

Civil Society

Non-governmental organizations and groups known as Civil Society play an increasingly influential role in the policies that govern the nation. These groups are made up of persons with special interests in areas such as labour, religion, environment, and other social issues. Belize has incorporated Civil Society into government by assigning three seats in the Senate to their representatives.

Start a scrap book using newspaper clippings of prominent court cases and follow the judicial process.

Divide the class in groups and have each group select a civil society organisation. Find out what their goals and projects are. Why it is important for civil society to participate in government? Present your findings to the class.

Chapter 14
The Economy of Belize

Economy is a term we use to describe the efficient allocation of **resources**. There are different types of resources: the land, labour and capital are the fundamental resources of an economy. The efficient allocation of resources is important in order to obtain the maximum return.

There are basically two methods by which resources are allocated: the first uses market forces which determine the price of goods and services. When goods are in abundance and readily available the price is low. When goods are scarce the price increases.

The second way in which resources are allocated is by the government trying to pre-determine how best the resources can be used. One of the important functions of governments is economic planning.

Governments need financial resources to function. The government makes much of the revenue it needs to manage the economy through taxation. Much of this revenue comes from import duties, sales tax, corporate and income tax, property tax and licences.

Often a country needs to borrow to undertake certain infrastructural projects. For example, the government of Belize

Read the definition of the term "economy". In your own words, explain the meaning of allocation of resources.

Explain different ways that a government's economic policies can influence the allocation of land.

Observe the fluctuation of price of an agricultural product and say which market forces influenced the prices of the product.

Belize's work force contributes to the growth of the economy.

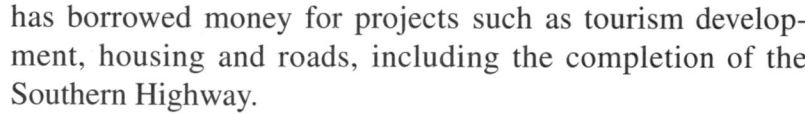

Karl Heusner Memorial Hospital.

The Hummingbird Highway.

has borrowed money for projects such as tourism development, housing and roads, including the completion of the Southern Highway.

Before independence, much of these funds were provided by Britain. Also, international agencies provide us with grants and aid with rates of interest lower than commercial banks. External assistance is becoming more difficult to obtain and the efficient management of our resources has become more important. External borrowing by the government can contribute to economic development; however, the funding must be spent wisely.

How is the gross revenue of a country used?

The Gross Revenue of a country is used to pay wages to government employees, to build infrastructure such as schools, roads and hospitals and also to pay foreign debt.

A country's Gross Domestic Product (GDP) is the value of all goods and services produced within the country's borders. Belize sells goods and services within the country and also exports goods and services to other parts of the world. The earnings from exports are used to pay for imports: food, clothing and other goods that come from foreign countries.

Why is Belize dependent on imported goods? Write down a list of measures that would help decrease the dependency on imported goods.

A country's balance of payment records transactions between people of that country and people in the rest of the world. It is important that small countries like Belize have a surplus in the balance of payment. This can be achieved by an increase in exports of goods and services and by direct foreign investment.

Imports and Exports

No country produces everything it needs. Those things which it lacks have to be bought from other countries. These are called imports. Exports are the goods a country sells to other countries.

Many of the goods consumed and used in Belize are imported from other countries. Belize is very dependent on imported goods. Although a variety of agricultural products are produced here, people still consume a lot of imported food. Other items are imported because Belize does not manufacture them.

The major imported foods are meat and dairy products, cereals, fruits and vegetables. Items like home appliances, electrical equipment, clothes and shoes are also imported. Traditionally, many of these items were bought from the U.S. Over the years, Belize has come to trade more with Mexico as well as other Caribbean and Central American countries.

Belize's economy depends heavily on a few exports. Its main products – sugar, bananas, citrus and marine products – make up 75 per cent of all domestic exports. This dependence makes the economy vulnerable to changes in international prices.

Most of our major exports are sold under preferential agreements at a price higher than the world market. Belize has preferencial treatment for sugar with the **European Union** (E.U.) and the U.S., and for bananas with the European Union. A quota is the amount a country can sell at a preferential price.

✎ *Make a list of goods consumed in your home in a week. Make two graphs showing locally produced and imported goods.*

✎ *Find out about Belize's major export products. Compare your list with a classmate.*

✎✎ *Make a list of non-traditional exports and say how they can contribute to the diversification of Belize's economy.*

Imported goods.

Bananas for export.

96

Like imports, exports were once most significant with Britain. More recently the U.S. has become our most important trading partner followed by countries of the E.U., the Caribbean and the Commonwealth.

Since 1980, non-traditional agricultural exports have increased. The most important are molasses and papaya. The amount of marine products that were exported increased as well, mostly due to the growth in shrimp farming. Shrimp is now exported to the U.S., the Caribbean Community and Central American countries.

Although forest products were very important in Belize's early history, their importance has steadily declined. There has been an increase in the export of value added local wood products.

Harvesting cane: a primary activity

The Three Levels of the Economy: Following Sugar Cane

Economic activities are normally divided into three types: primary, secondary and tertiary. In sugar we will see an example of all three.

In northern Belize, a farmer has grown a large crop of cane. He has chosen the right kind of soil to plant it in. He has had to depend on good weather for his crop to grow. Finally, it is ready to harvest. His workers cut the cane, load it into trucks and drive it to a factory near Orange Walk.

At the factory, workers unload the cane. At the sugar mill the cane is processed into many different kinds of products: white and brown sugar and molasses. A large part of the production is exported and some is consumed locally.

Tower Hill sugar mill, Orange Walk.

From here, the sugar goes to different places. Some of it is packed in small bags, and goes to grocery stores. Some is packed and shipped to foreign countries. Some goes to other factories, that use it in making products like rum and in the processing of other foods. Meanwhile, the company has hired designers and other professionals. They will make sure the sugar sells by making an attractive package. Finally, your mother brings home a bag of sugar from the store and you put it on your cereal.

Make a list of activities for each one of the sectors of the economy.

We have just followed sugar through the three levels of the economy in Belize: the primary, the secondary and the tertiary. All three sectors are related to each other, and each depends on the others.

Give two examples of products which involve the three sectors of Belize's economy.

Papayas are a non-traditional crop.

Packing papayas for export.

✍ Give two reasons for the importance of agriculture in the economy of a country.

✍ Draw a map of Belize. Use symbols to show the areas where the major agricultural crops are grown.

The primary sector uses the natural resources of Belize, just as our cane farmer used the land. Through agriculture, forestry, fishing and mining, the primary sector provides the raw materials that will later be processed. This part of our economy employs over one-fourth of Belize's labour force.

The secondary sector is responsible for manufacturing and processing. People in factories process the raw materials, like cane, into products which we can buy in the store, like sugar.

The tertiary sector consists of services. When our farmer's sugar was packaged and marketed, people were providing a service. Services are provided for the primary and secondary levels of the economy. They can also cover a wide range of fields, like insurance, financing, hotel and restaurant industries and tourism.

Using Our Natural Resources: The Primary Sector

Since the early days of the settlement the use of natural resources has been the primary activity. The economy in Belize is directly linked to our natural resources. Agriculture, fishing and forestry, as well as tourism, all depend on these resources for food and income. Because of this, the conservation and proper management of land and resources is very important.

Agriculture

Agriculture is the backbone of our economy. Not only does agriculture produce the most wealth and employ the most people, it also feeds our country. For this reason, the government tries to assist farmers by providing technical assistance, incentives and encouraging exports.

One of the most important crops is sugar cane. In 2000 there were 9,040 registered cane farmers in Belize, mostly in small farms in the Orange Walk and Corozal districts. Another important crop is citrus, with the highest concentration in the Stann Creek Valley. Banana production has dramatically increased. Many banana plantations are found in the Stann Creek and Toledo districts. Citrus and banana plantations are often large and employ many people.

All of these crops are important export crops. Yet many different kinds of crops are grown for domestic use in the country. Belize is almost self-sufficient in corn, rice and beans. The farms that produce these crops range from small milpas to large mechanized estates.

Belize is trying to diversify its agriculture. The reason for this is because dependence on one or a few crops is risky. If the crops do not do well or their price falls, the economy will suffer. If there are many different crops, the failure will not affect the economy as much.

Farmers have diversified their crops by growing things like papaya, soybeans and peanuts. Some cacao is also grown. Another type of crop grown only for domestic use is vegetables. These include tomatoes, cabbage, peppers, cucumbers, lettuce and carrots. Vegetables are only sold to local markets or used by the farmer. The weather and soil in Belize limits vegetable crops. They may only be grown from November to February if water is not available to irrigate the land. During the dry season many vegetables are imported from Mexico and Guatemala.

Belizean agriculture also includes livestock. This produces beef, pork, poultry and eggs. In the last few decades the country has become self-sufficient in beef, pork, poultry and eggs. Beef cattle are important for the economies of Orange Walk and Cayo.

The Mennonites produce much of the grain crops such as corn and sorghum.

✐✐ *In groups, research one non-traditional agricultural crop. Describe the process from planting to harvesting and marketing.*

✐✐ *Interview a family engaged in subsistence farming.*

Small farmers supply the country with fruit and vegetables.

A chicken farm at Spanish Lookout.

Subsistence farming.

✍ Why is the fishing industry a vital part of the economy?

✍✍ List the six fishing cooperatives in Belize and locate them on the map.

Small farms grow rice, corn, beans, vegetables, bananas, plantain, citrus, sugarcane and fruit. They also raise cattle, pigs, poultry and bees. Usually they are owned by families who also do all the work. They take care of all aspects of the farm, from seeding the crop to selling it at the market.

Some groups of people have particular agricultural practices. The Garinagu on the sea coast often grow cassava and supplement their diet with fish. The Maya in southern Toledo often plant milpas and rice that provide them with food. The Mennonites are the largest and most efficient farmers in Belize. They supply Belize with 90 per cent of its poultry and eggs. They also grow a large portion of corn, rice, beans and animal feed. Mennonites live communally. They pool their resources to farm, which makes it easier to buy equipment and makes it less risky. Most Mennonite farms are mechanized.

The Fishing Industry

The fishing industry is a vital part of our economy contributing about 3.7 per cent to our Gross Domestic Product (GDP), according to 2001 statistics. In 2001, the estimated dollar value of this industry was BZ$ 49.9 million. Recently there has been a decline of 7.5 per cent. Contributing factors to the decline have been natural disasters and increased competition from Central American countries.

Fishing has grown from a **subsistence** activity to a commercial export activity to places like the U.S., Europe and the Caribbean. The export market opened in the 1920s, with lobster and conch being the top exported products. These products have remained important parts of catches for fishermen in Belize. Shrimp is also a valued fishery product. Fin-fish, while popular on the local market, represents only a small portion of our exports.

Most fishing takes place inside the Barrier Reef and around Glovers', Turneffe and Lighthouse Reef. Fishermen come from all along the coast and cayes of Belize to fish. In Sarteneja, San Pedro, Caye Caulker, Dangriga, Placencia and Punta Gorda, residents rely heavily on fishing, both to earn a living and to provide protein in their diets.

Protected Areas, like the Hol Chan Marine Reserve, provide a safe haven where organisms like lobsters can feed, grow and reproduce without much disturbance. In shallow waters in the north, they are caught in nets, and traps. Lobsters are caught by spearing in the deeper water of the south.

Before the opening of the export market, lobster, not yet a prized catch, was thrown away at sea. But now that it has a value of up to BZ$ 28.00 per pound, fishermen try to sell as much as they can catch. This could easily lead to over-harvesting and therefore the Ministry of Agriculture and the Fisheries Department have regulations in place to protect all our fisheries, including the lobster fishery.

Lobsters cannot be caught from the 15th of February to the 14th of June both days inclusive. Any lobster caught must be over four ounces. This allows young lobsters to mature to adulthood and enables adults to reproduce.

The development of fishing cooperatives has helped Belize to become successful in fishing. They have also helped fishermen to unite as a group and have more power. By combining their resources, fishermen were able to buy bigger boats. This allowed them to go further out to the sea to new fishing areas, as well as accommodating them for longer trips. The first cooperative began on Caye Caulker. Today, there are four

A shrimp-packing plant, Belize District.

On a map locate Belize's main fishing areas and main fishing communities.

Research and make a drawing of the main species of fish caught in Belizean waters.

Find out about the marine products that are available in your community.

Conch is also an important export commodity.

Fishing boats by the Haulover Creek in Belize City.

A Belize City fish market.

functional ones countrywide. The Belize Fishermen's Cooperative Association (BFCA), an umbrella organization for cooperatives in Belize, represents their interest and the interests of fishermen who belong to the cooperatives. Cooperatives contribute 80 per cent of production in the fishing industry.

There is only price control on ungutted fish but none for other fisheries products. In addition, the government requires that five per cent of products taken to co-operatives are sold locally.

In the last two decades, the rapid growth of tourism on islands like Ambergris Caye and Caye Caulker has made fishing less important to the local economy. Many people who used to fish for a living now use their boats for tourist-based activities.

While fishing has been contributing less to the local economy on the cayes, it has been contributing more in gross dollar value to the overall economy of Belize. In 2001, the export earnings alone were over 66 million dollars. As traditional marine resources become scarce, new products like aquarium plants and fish, seaweed and king crab, are becoming popular in the industry. **Aquaculture** specially shrimp farming is playing an increasingly important role.

Today with the growing aquaculture business, the introduction of processed products, like smoked and salted fish products, particularly on the export market, the industry continues to grow.

Forestry

The forest industry was the basis of Belize's economy from the beginning of the settlement but it no longer has the importance it used to have. In fact, some hardwoods are now imported because of the poor quality of local lumber.

At present, 79 per cent of our land is covered by forest. However, with large scale logging now taking place in some parts of the country our forests and protected areas are being threatened. Demand for land and a fast increase in population is also putting our pristine forests in danger.

Find out about the main types of lumber available to builders in your community. Find out how much the price of mahogany and other woods have increased in the past 10 years.

102

A sawmill in operation.

Government restricts the export of raw lumber

More and more of the forest is being cut down and replaced by large farming ventures such as citrus farms and other commercial agriculture. More and more people are trespassing and cutting in the country's forest reserves, breaking the laws for protected areas.

There are still a small amount of people employed in forestry. Most of them cut softwoods like pines in the Granite Basin near the Maya Mountains and on the coastal plains. Then the logs go to sawmills to provide lumber for the local market. Recently there has been a renewed interest in chicle harvesting.

Lumber ready for export.

Forests are threatened by many natural hazards like hurricanes which often knock down large trees. Fires are also a big threat, as they can destroy hundreds of acres of prime timber. Forest land is cleared more often for agriculture, towns and cities, and rural populations. Recently, the pine beetle has destroyed large numbers of pine trees in the Mountain Pine Ridge area.

✐✐ *Make a list of commercial species presently logged in Belize. Find out how many years the trees take to mature.*

Forests are a **renewable resource**. If we replant areas that have been logged they can continue to provide us with lumber. To make sure we have enough timber, the forestry sector today attempts to replant areas that have been logged. This will ensure that the forests are a sustainable resource.

✐ *List the main reasons for the decline of the forestry industry in Belize.*

The dam on the Macal River.

Orange processing plant at Pomona, Stann Creek Valley.

The Secondary Sector: Transforming Resources into Manufactured Goods

The second part of the economy transforms our resources into useful goods. These goods can be exported or used in the country. Manufacturing also uses raw materials from other countries to produce goods.

Belize is not a major industrial or manufacturing country. One reason for this is because our domestic demand is small. Another constraint is our small labour force.

Belize is better suited to medium and small manufacturing. Belize's main manufactured products are citrus concentrate and fresh orange juice, and sugar products. Other manufactured agricultural products are dairy products, flour, beverages, meats and dehydrated fruit. Smaller operations manufacture products like pepper sauce, jams, peanut butter, fresh juices and yogurt. Wood products such as veneer, plywood and furniture are becoming more important.

Many manufacturers are centred in Belize City. One of the more important industries is the garment industry, which makes clothes from imported materials. Cigarettes are also manufactured from imported tobacco, and other factories make soap and oils. The construction industry has become important for the secondary sector and employs a large number of people that builds **infrastructure** as well as houses.

The supply of water and electricity are also part of the secondary manufacturing industry. Belize Electricity Limited is in charge of distributing electricity. The main power station for Belize City is at Ladyville. During the rainy season, the hydroelectric plant in the Vaca Falls area is meant to be capable of providing 100 per cent of the electricity needs of Benque Viejo del Carmen, San Ignacio, Belmopan and Belize City.

Tertiary Sector: The Service Industries

The tertiary sector is also known as the service sector since it provides the services a country needs. Commerce, communications and the service-oriented industries such as restaurants and hotels are tertiary sector activities. People who provide

Which economic activities are included in the secondary sector?

Write a short composition explaining why Belize is not a manufacturing country.

Research and describe a manufacturing process.

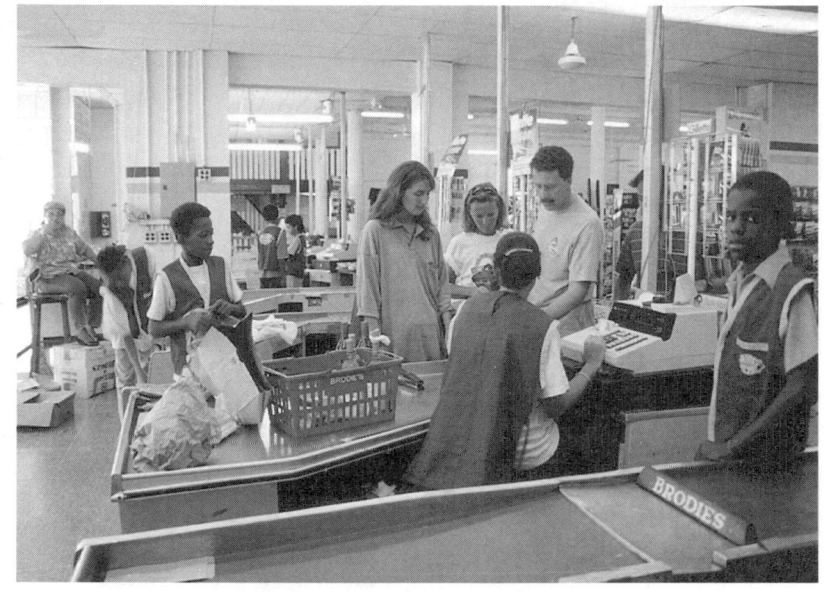
Commerce is a tertiary sector activity.

Auto-mechanics provide an important service.

News broadcast, Belize City.

services include anybody from professionals like teachers or government employees, to unskilled workers. In 2000 the tertiary sector produced earnings of 61.5 per cent of the GDP of the country.

Communication Technology: Welcome to the Future

Communications promote the exchange of ideas and have a great influence on everyday life. Telephones, television and computers can inform us of events outside the country, as well as remind us of our common heritage and way of life. Services like police, the Forest Department and airports all depend on modern technology for communication. Businesses and schools profit from it too. Modern communications save time, energy and money.

The cost of some of the new technology means that not everybody can use it. A few areas in Belize are still not served by telephone or electricity because their remoteness makes installation very costly.

Belize Telecommunications Ltd (BTL) has a monopoly to operate in Belize until the year 2003. Other than the regular telephone service, this private business offers services which include cellular phones, faxes and electronic mail. E-mail,

✎ Which economic activities are included in the tertiary sector?

✎✎ In groups make a list of professions that belong to the tertiary sector. Explain why.

✎✎ Discuss the various modern technologies that help communication.

🖊🖊 *Why is infrastructure important to a country?*

🖊🖊 *In the communications map of the Atlas observe and discuss Belize's road network.*

🖊 *On a map of Belize locate Belize's main ports.*

connects users of computers through lightning-fast communication. The Internet allows computer users to send and collect information all over the world. These services connect individuals as well as businesses and institutions through telephone lines and computers.

A good infrastructure is very important for the economic growth of the country. A country's infrastructure includes roads, bridges, ports, telephones, radio and television. It also includes electricity, water supply and sewerage. Infrastructure is an essential part of any economy. Manufactured goods must be taken to their destination by land, sea or air. In Belize, the tourism industry also requires good infrastructure like roads and airports so visitors can reach our resorts.

Because of its landscape, until recently many communities in Belize remained isolated and inaccessible by road. Today the major roads in Belize are passable in all seasons. There is a total of 3,026 kilometres of roads in the country. Of these, 452 kilometres are major highways.

The main airport and shipping port are located in Belize City. The harbour of Belize City does not have deep waters. Large ships, therefore, must anchor a mile offshore and cargo has to be transported in and out by smaller boats. Deep water ports are found in Big Creek and Commerce Bight. These ports are used for the export of citrus and bananas.

Bridge construction.

Philip Goldson International Airport.

Tourism

Tourism is the most important industry in the service sector of Belize. It is also the largest single contributor to the economy, with 21.4 per cent of GDP. In 2001, 195,955 people visited Belize.

A jungle resort in Northern Belize.

The tourism industry has both advantages and disadvantages. It creates jobs for the Belizean people because it supports one of every four jobs. It represents 17.7 percent of the National Gross Domestic Product (GDP) and provides foreign exchange earnings. However, the increase of visitors might increase the danger of environmental damage. It can also create economic problems for the local people, such as inflation of prices and inaccessibility of land. Tourism promotes the natural and historical heritage of Belize and it strengthens the cultural exchange between Belizeans and visitors, but it can also promote cultural alienation, drugs, and prostitution.

The Ministry of Tourism is the main body that is responsible for policies and activities of tourism. The Belize Tourism Board is the executing agency of the Ministry of Tourism and it is responsible for the marketing and development of the tourism sector. Some of the service providers of tourism are the travel agencies, hotels, and guest houses, transportation providers, and restaurants.

A domestic airline.

What is a Tourist?

A tourist is a person taking a trip during their holiday. There are three types of tourist: national tourists, regional tourists, and international tourists.

In which way does tourism benefit Belize and its people?

Tourists visit many places in Belize. Their visit depends on their main interest, these may be marine activities such as snorkeling and diving in the Barrier Reef or, visiting the cayes and atolls. Terrestrial activities may include navigating our many rivers, caving and visiting our beautiful archaeological sites. Since Belize is a small country they are often able to enjoy both.

Debate the positive and negative aspects of tourism.

What is Tourism?

Tourism is the organization and operation of holidays as a commercial enterprise. It encompasses both the activities of people and the facilities and services created for them.

A beach resort in San Pedro, Ambergris Caye.

There are two types of tourism: mass tourism and ecotourism. The type of tourism in Belize is ecotourism.

1. Mass tourism – consists of large scale development that provides large amounts of visitors with services and activities in a given area. Cancun and Miami are examples of mass tourism.

2. Ecotourism – is defined as responsible travel that conserves the natural, social and cultural environment and sustains the well-being of the local people. This type of tourism is the one that occurs in Belize and Costa Rica.

Ecotourism can focus on different activities:

Adventure Tourism – consists of participating in adventurous activities, such as snorkeling, fishing, boating, canoeing, hiking, biking, camping, bird watching, caving, horseback riding, and archaeological touring.

Cultural Tourism – consists of discovering about the social and cultural activities, such as religion, dance, food, and other customs. It also includes the visiting or studying of archaeological sites and museums.

Rural Tourism – promotes the creation of local enterprises by communities using local resources as tourist attractions. Some places where this takes place are: Crooked Tree, Bermudian Landing, Sarteneja, Consejo and Maya villages in Southern Belize.

Discuss and write an essay of the advantages of ecotourism to Belize.

Collect brochures, adds and newspaper clippings. Make a scrap book of eco- tourist destinations in Belize.

108

The Labour Force: Employment and Unemployment

In order to have a growing economy, a country must have a productive and skilled labour force.

Nearly half of the population in Belize is under 15 years old. As you and your school mates grow older, there will be more competition for jobs. Already there are high numbers of young people who do not find jobs. This measurement of people working is called employment. Unemployment in the country as a whole, however, has gone down in the last two decades. The amount of women working out of the home, in particular, has more than tripled since the 1970s. Other factors influence employment. The migration of people into Belize has meant that there are more people who can work and more competition for jobs.

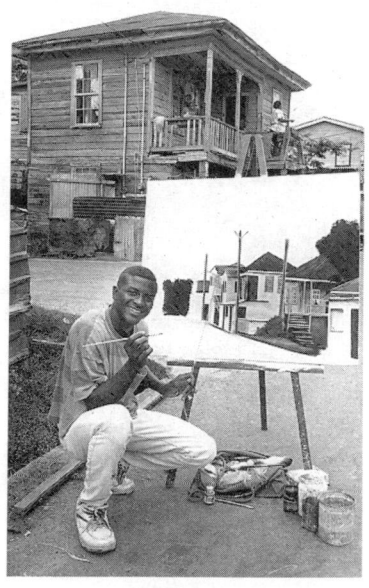

Artists make an important contribution to society.

In 2000, the service sector accounted for 55 per cent of total employment. The manufacturing sector accounted for 17 per cent. The percentage of Belize's labour force employed in agriculture, forestry and fishing is 27.2 and they are the industries that employ the most people.

Many agricultural workers from Central America come to work in the sugar industry in the north and the banana and citrus industries in the south. One of the things that attracts people from other countries to work in Belize is higher wages.

Higher wages in developed countries also cause Belizeans to travel there for work. Minimum wages in the U.S. are about four times higher than in Belize and there may also be better opportunities. When skilled people leave Belize to work in other countries they may personally benefit, but the country loses their help. Trained professionals like doctors and teachers are essential in the development process of a country.

The economy of Belize is built by the work of its labour force. What is important is to increase our nation's wealth by using both our natural and human resources. Education and creativity are essential in increasing this wealth.

Find out about the jobs most commonly found in your community.

Interview a worker. Write a description of his or her job. Find out their qualifications and work experience. Are they satisfied with their job? Share the findings with your class.

In groups, find out about the unemployment situation in Belize. Share your findings with your class.

CARIBBEAN

Part Three
Belize in the Region

SITUATED ON A NARROW STRETCH of land that joins North and South America, Belize's coast looks out to the Caribbean Sea. These two factors make Belize a part of both Central America and the Caribbean.

The **isthmus** of Central America not only divides North and South America, but draws the line between the Pacific and Atlantic Oceans as well. Geographically, Central America begins in the Mexican Isthmus of Tehuantepec and ends in Panama. It consists of seven countries: Belize, Guatemala, El Salvador, Honduras, Nicaragua, Costa Rica and Panama.

SEA

The islands of the Caribbean are linked to Central America through a partially submerged mountain chain. Beginning in Venezuela, the chain runs through the Lesser Antilles to Hispaniola, then splits with one mountain range running through Cuba and the other to Honduras.

The hundreds of islands in the West Indies range from the large island of Cuba to tiny mountain tops poking out of the sea like Saba. Together, they form an archipelago, a chain of islands over 2,400 kilometres long.

The Caribbean includes many islands and mainland countries with shorelands in the Caribbean Sea. These nations also share history and culture. Recently they have begun to celebrate and strengthen those ties.

Festival del Caribe in Cancun.

Chapter 15
Belize: Where Central America Meets the Caribbean

In the 16th and 17th centuries, the Americas were colonised by European powers. Most of Central America was colonised by Spain.

The islands of the Caribbean were controlled by four major powers: Spain, Britain, France and Holland. The nations of Europe were often at war with each other. Because of this, British territories maintained political and economic links mostly among themselves. Even after independence, many nations continued this practice.

Belize was colonised by the British and so our culture is similar to the English-speaking Caribbean. But many of our people have also immigrated from Mexico and Central America, further enriching our culture.

Communication Between Regions

Much of the communication between countries in the region was initially through marine travel. Settlements by Europeans began near the coast where they landed. It was often easier to travel by sea than overland through dense forest.

This pattern continued well into the 20th century. Communication between the coastal settlements of Yucatan and Central America strengthened ties within the region. Belize first developed maritime links with coastal settlements along the Caribbean coast of Mexico, Guatemala and Honduras. Links with Caribbean islands such as Barbados, Jamaica and Trinidad and Tobago were also developed through colonial contact.

Highways and roads were and still are important for communication between Central American countries. Where there is little population or bad roads, contact with parts of Central America becomes difficult.

Dominican traditional dress reflects African and European influences.

✏️ In which ways is Belize similar to other countries in the Caribbean?

✏️ Make a class mural. Trace and label a map of Central America and the Caribbean. Find postcards, newspaper clippings, postage stamps or photographs, or make drawings. Paste them in your mural.

Coastal travelling within the region.

Why has Belize been so isolated from Central America?

Belize is the only Central American country that is not connected by the Pan American Highway, which runs from Ciudad Juárez on the Mexico-U.S. border to Panama City. In the north, Belize is connected to Mexico by a major highway to the state of Quintana Roo. The only road from Belize to Central America is through Guatemala's Petén region. Because it is usually in bad condition, it is not heavily travelled.

One of the reasons for Belize's isolation from Central America has been the lack of development and low population of Guatemala's Petén Department. Many Belizeans travel to the border town of Melchor de Mencos for day-trips, but few travel beyond. However, educational links with Guatemala are strong. Every year, Guatemalan-trained doctors, architects and engineers contribute to Belize's development. Our appreciation of Guatemala is increased as we share in its experience.

Majestic Tikal, just a short distance from our western border.

There are no roads that cross Belize's southern border. The major link is by boat from Punta Gorda. This service connects Belize to Guatemala and also to Honduras.

On Belize's northern border, the Mexican state of Quintana Roo has developed quickly. Many Belizeans continue to travel to this area for shopping, medical treatment, business or holidays. All of these increasing links with Mexico have helped us to appreciate our neighbour's culture.

Immigration check point at Santa Elena, northern Belize.

Airplanes have succeeded in making connections where highways could not. Pan American Airlines began to fly out of the U.S. in the 1920s, bringing mail and passengers to Yucatan and Central American countries. Transport became quicker and more efficient. Today, however, flights between Central America and the Caribbean are limited.

As a member of the Commonwealth, Belize maintains strong links with the Caribbean. Belize is a member of Caribbean regional institutions such as CARICOM, the Caribbean Development Bank, the University of the West Indies and the Association of Caribbean States.

Modern buildings in the industrious northern city of Monterrey.

Mexico

The border between Mexico and Belize follows the Rio Hondo in the north of our country. The geography and villages on both sides of the border are very similar. The physical resemblance of those who live there is also very striking. This is because most of the people who live here are of Maya origin. In this area, it is common to hear the Maya language as well as English and Spanish.

Along with the Maya in the south of Mexico, there are more than 60 indigenous groups living in different areas of Mexico. These groups conserve their many different languages and customs. Although the official language of Mexico is Spanish, there are many other languages spoken. The culture of the Mexican people is like a great mosaic, with many contrasts from region to region.

The land and the environment are as diverse as the people. Mexico is a country so large that it has mountains always covered with snow, extensive deserts, long rivers and many lakes, lush tropical forests and areas with very poor soil, like the Yucatan Peninsula.

The west coast of Mexico faces the Pacific Ocean, while the east faces the Atlantic Ocean, forming the Gulf of Mexico. Mexico also has another peninsula in the north, Baja

Name the different ways in which Belizeans interact with the country of Mexico. Tell how we benefit from these interactions.

Trace a map of Mexico showing the main physical features, states and state capitals.

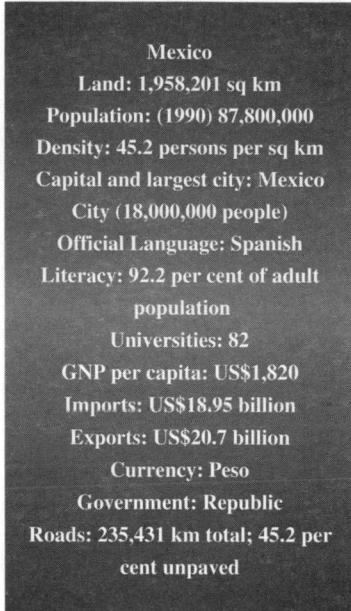

Write a short essay saying in which ways Mexico is similar to Belize and in which ways it is different.

Downtown Mérida, Mexico.

California. Between this Peninsula and the mainland we find the Sea of Cortés.

Mexico's northern border stretches 3,000 kilometres along the U.S. Together with the U.S. and Canada, Mexico is a part of North America.

Mexico is considered a leader among Latin American countries. Latin America extends from the Rio Bravo to Tierra de Fuego. The countries of Latin America have in common their colonial history and a similar level of development. But what unites them is their common culture. The people have very similar customs, and the same music, movies, writers and artists are popular throughout the area. Today television keeps people informed about the latest developments in the countries of the region. Although Belize's official language is not Spanish, Belize is also a part of Latin America.

Thirty per cent of the Mexican population live in rural areas and work the land. The majority of these farmers are poor, and produce essential food like corn, beans, pumpkin, chile, and many different fruits and vegetables. Yet there are also many who produce food for sale and export. Mexico's main exports are coffee, cocoa, cotton, tropical fruits, flowers and vegetables. Cattle ranching is also an important activity. Many farms sell cattle and maintain extensive pastures.

Since the 1950s Mexican industries have been supported by the government. In this way, the government intended to produce merchandise for export. This was how Mexico's industrial economy grew. Now the country manufactures many goods for export. This sector of the economy has replaced agriculture in economic importance.

Oil is Mexico's main export. It has helped greatly in the development of the country. In 1938 the Mexican government nationalised the oil industry. Private or foreign companies are not allowed to operate in this sector of the Mexican industry. Resources such as natural gas, oil and petrochemicals, help pay for the development of infrastructure, health services and other social and educational programmes for all Mexicans.

Tourism is also an important aspect of the Mexican economy. Major tourist destinations like beaches, archaeological sites and colonial cities have been developed for tourism. Besides visitors from the U.S., Mexico is also visited by many Canadians, Europeans, Asians and a growing number of Latin Americans. Mexico's arts and crafts, music and traditional dances, as well as its cuisine, are additional attractions for visitors.

One of the major problems Mexico is facing is the high population density of its cities. This has made it difficult to provide enough public services. Problems like pollution, crime and migration are on the increase. Migration from rural to urban areas makes the shanty towns around the cities continue to grow. Seventy per cent of Mexico's population live in the cities.

What do countries in Latin America have in common?

The situation in Mexico City is especially critical. It has a population of 18 million people, one-fifth of the total population.

Give a brief summary of Mexico's economy. Find out about Mexico's participation in CARIFTA.

Since the end of the 1970s the Mexican economy has had constant difficulties. Social conflicts are becoming more frequent and serious. The relative stability in Mexico for many years is explained by the fact that only one party, the PRI, held power without losing one election for many years. With much social discontent, such as the recent armed conflict in Chiapas, and more political competition, the PRI has recently lost many elections.

Find out some of the major tourist attractions in the States of Yucatan and Quintana Roo.

At one point, Mexico claimed a portion of northern Belize, but this claim was dropped many years ago. Today the two countries work in close collaboration and since independence Mexico's solidarity with Belize has strengthened.

The tourist resort of Cancun, Quintana Roo, Mexico.

Snorkeling in the clear waters of Isla Mujeres, Quintana Roo.

Chapter 16
The Land and People of Central America

The Land

Central America is a narrow 3,218 kilometres long isthmus that connects North and South America. Its major feature is a mountain chain that runs from Southern Mexico to Panama, reaching heights above 3,657 metres. This mountain range receives many different names along the way, like Isabela in Nicaragua and Talamanca in Costa Rica.

This mountain chain that runs along the Pacific coast is part of the same mountain range that begins in Alaska and ends in Tierra de Fuego.

From the Mexican border to Costa Rica, a chain of volcanoes stretches 1,300 kilometres. Some of these volcanoes are still active. These volcanoes appear along a line where two tectonic plates collide. Because of this fault, Mexico, Guatemala, El Salvador and Nicaragua have always been severely affected by earthquakes and volcanic eruptions.

✏ *Trace a map showing the narrow isthmus of Central America in relation to North and South America.*

✏ *Why are most countries in Central America affected by earthquakes and volcanic eruptions?*

Wearing protective clothing, scientists are able to study volcanoes more closely.

Lake Atitlán in Guatemala.

The west coast of Central America is bathed by the waters of the Pacific Ocean, while the east coast faces the Atlantic Ocean.

Central America has a tropical climate. But highland areas of Guatemala and Costa Rica have much cooler climates. The coastal lowlands are hot and humid. On the Caribbean side hurricanes occasionally produce major damage. The year is divided into wet and dry seasons.

Rivers in Central America are short. Several of them serve as borders between countries. These include the Rio Hondo, the Sarstoon River, the Rio Coco, Rio San Juan and Rio Usumacinta. Lake Nicaragua is the largest lake in the area and in it a rare species of fresh water shark is found.

Locate the following rivers: Rio Hondo, Sarstoon River, Rio Coco, Rio San Juan and Rio Usumacinta. Say which countries they divide.

The people

Central America has a population of approximately 24 million. When Columbus landed in Central America in 1502, the area was populated by many different indigenous groups. When the Spanish arrived, wars, new diseases and harsh slavery killed great numbers of them. Today, most Central Americans are mestizos. But there is also a large number of indigenous people as well. Africans were brought to Central America as slaves and now make up a significant percentage of the population. There are also a small number of European, Asian and North American settlers and their descendants.

In Guatemala, indigenous people make up about 50 per cent of the population.

Spanish is the main language in Central America. English is spoken in Belize and in some parts of Panama, Nicaragua, Guatemala and Costa Rica. About two million people speak one of many variations of English Creole along the Atlantic coast of Central America.

Write an essay that explains the ethnic composition of Central American people. Discuss it with your class.

Maya languages are spoken in parts of Guatemala, Honduras and Belize. In Belize, Honduras, Guatemala and Nicaragua Garifuna is also spoken.

Most of the mestizo population lives along the Pacific coast. Other groups, such as the Garinagu, black and Miskito populations live along Central America's Atlantic coast.

History

Find out which areas of Central America were settled by the British?

Find out the date in which Central America became independent from Spain.

The National Palace in Guatemala City: the symbol of a long history of military dictatorships.

Before the arrival of the Spanish, Central America was the home of various indigenous peoples, most notably the Maya. The Maya's advanced civilization stretched from the Yucatan peninsula to northern Honduras and El Salvador. From the 16th century, following Columbus' landing on the continent, the Spanish fought the Maya, claimed the land and controlled the region.

The British, meanwhile, were using piracy and war to establish their own colonies. In the middle of the 17th century, British pirates settled on the Mosquito Coast in present day Nicaragua, and the Bay of Honduras, which became Belize.

The struggle for independence from Spanish rule in other Central American regions began early in the 19th century. In 1821, the countries of the region formed the Central American Federation, with San Salvador as its capital. By 1838, the attempt collapsed. The new independent countries struggled for economic survival.

Because of Central America's strategic link between the Pacific and Atlantic Oceans, the U.S. began to take an interest in the region. In the 19th century, it was often easier to travel from the west coast to the east coast of the U.S. by first sailing south down to Central America. Then travelers would cross the narrow isthmus by land, and return to the opposite coast by

Colonial and indigenous presence in Guatemala.

sailing north. A shortcut through Central America by waterways was finally opened with the Panama Canal in 1914.

The presence of U.S. multinational companies in the region began towards the end of the 19th century. They established large plantations for the growing of tropical fruits like bananas, and exploited forest resources like lumber and chicle. North American companies such as the United Fruit Company hired peasants for cheap labour. The money the companies made mostly went back to the U.S.

Throughout its history, the majority of Central American countries were affected by dictatorships, corruption, exploitation and civil wars. The unfair concentration of most of the land and capital in the hands of a few families led people to fight for their rights.

Since the 1960s, guerrilla movements began to fight oppressive governments. The ruling military regimes were supported by powerful businesses and large land-owners. Guerrilla wars were begun by peasant and student movements in Guatemala, Nicaragua and El Salvador.

In order to protect their businesses in the region, the U.S. supported the military governments in their fight with popular movements.

Civil wars, therefore, have caused thousands of people to seek refuge in other countries. Many of these refugees have come to Belize. Today, under the observation of the United Nations, Central American countries struggle for real peace. This decade has seen the end of military regimes and dictatorships in Central America, and a slow return to democracy is taking place.

The Guatemalan claim to Belize created fear and hostility on the part of many Belizeans towards Guatemala. But in the late 1970s, Latin American countries, including most of Central America, gave their support to Belize's independence.

Belize's history has been different from the rest of Central America. Ours is the only country that speaks English as a national language, and some of our customs are different as well. Because of our colonial past, links with the British Caribbean region were, and still are, strong. Our connections

What were the reasons for the U.S.'s interest in Central America?

What have been some of the causes of instability in Central America? Why?

Why is the history of Belize different from the rest of Central America? In which way it is similar?

Name some of the consequences of civil war in Central America.

During the 70's the majority of Nicaraguans supported the revolt against Somoza's rule.

121

✏ *Give a brief summary of the people and economy of Guatemala.*

✏✏ *Write a short composition comparing the history, population and economy of Belize and Guatemala.*

The Petén department is a sparsely populated lowland tropical region.

with Central America were slower to develop. Belize was, and still is, the least populated country in Central America.

But beneath the surface, Belize shares much in common with all of Central America. All of its people have suffered under colonialism, slavery and oppression. Connections between people of all nations remain strong throughout the region.

Guatemala

The southern half of Guatemala consists of mountains and plateaus. The northern portion, called the Petén, is lowland covered by forest. Ancient Maya civilization flourished in this region of Guatemala before the arrival of the Spanish. The site of Tikal is one of the best examples of an ancient Maya city in Central America.

Approximately 50 per cent of Guatemala's 10 million people are Maya. The remainder are mestizo. The majority of the population live in the highland areas of the south. This area is also where most earthquakes happen. The official language of Guatemala is Spanish, but over 20 Maya languages are spoken. Almost 60 per cent of Guatemalans live in rural areas. These are largely the poor indigenous people of the country. Only 25 per cent of people living outside of cities have access to health services. In rural areas, only 43 per cent are provided with safe drinking water, compared with 92 per cent in cities and towns.

Guatemala's economy consists of agriculture, industry, mining and tourism. Agriculture is the most important activity. But many poor peasants farm to provide food only for their families. They also work on the large coffee and cotton plantations. Coffee is the main export in Guatemala. Guatemala is one of the most industrialized nations in Central America and it has large deposits of oil.

Since its independence, Guatemala has most often been governed by the military allied with a few wealthy landowners. Land and wealth are concentrated in the hands of a few. In the 1980s, civil war broke out between the military and destitute and landless peasants. After many thousands of deaths and changes of government, constitutional democracy was finally established.

122

Guatemala's first capital, Antigua Guatemala, was destroyed by an earthquake.

During the years of civil unrest, an indigenous leader, Rigoberta Menchú, worked for peace in her nation. In 1990, she was awarded the Nobel Peace Prize for her efforts.

Guatemala once claimed that Belize belonged to it. In 1983 it changed its claim to only the southern part of Belize. This part would have given Guatemala access to the Atlantic Ocean. Today, the dispute over the border has not yet been resolved but does not greatly affect relations between the two countries.

✏️✏️*Research and write a short essay on the life of Rigoberta Menchú.*

✏️✏️*Look at a detailed map of El Salvador and identify its main physical regions.*

El Salvador

El Salvador is both the smallest and most densely populated of the Central American countries. It is also the only Central American country with no Caribbean coast. El Salvador can be divided into three major physical regions: a tropical region on the Pacific, a central upland of valleys and plateaus, and a mountainous north. There are more than 20 active volcanoes in the country. Major earthquakes also cause damage. The most recent affected the capital of San Salvador in 1986.

Ninety per cent of the people are mestizos; only 10 per cent are indigenous. Before the Spanish conquest, the area was inhabited by the Pipil.

The nation's land and wealth belongs to a few rich families. Only two per cent of the population owns 60 per cent of the land. Land pressure has been the major cause of conflict in El

The catholic church was sympathetic to the popular movements during El Salvador's long civil war.

123

The volcanic sandy beaches of El Salvador's Pacific coast.

What major social problems have prompted many Salvadoreans to leave their country?

Write a short essay about coffee cultivation in El Salvador.

Drying coffee beans in El Salvador.

Salvador. War has killed 75,000 people since 1980 and caused US$ 2 billion worth of damage.

In January 1992, a peace agreement was signed between the government and the guerrilla movement. Today, land reform programmes try to alleviate unfair land ownership.

The economic activities in El Salvador consist of agriculture and manufacturing. Coffee is the leading crop, followed by cotton, sugar and shrimp. Rice and corn are grown for local consumption. The environment of this country is very damaged. The forest has almost disappeared, and erosion and pollution are serious problems. Much of these environmental problems are the result of overpopulation and the civil war.

Because of the violence and overpopulation, many people have chosen to leave El Salvador to live in other countries of the region, including Belize. These hard-working immigrants have helped Belize's agricultural development. Today, their children are fully integrated into the social and educational life of the country.

Honduras

The land in Honduras is very mountainous, with narrow plains that run along both Caribbean and Pacific coasts. Two major mountain ranges running east to west divide Honduras into halves. Its rugged terrain has created problems for transportation and made rural areas difficult to reach.

About 70 per cent of the population live in the mountain valleys. Spanish is the official language. The population is mostly mestizo, with smaller numbers of indigenous people, who live in the west near the Guatemalan border, as well as other racial groups. The Garifuna population lives mainly on the Caribbean coast. There are large numbers of refugees from neighbouring Central American countries.

Since Honduras' independence in 1821, there have been numerous coups and changes of government. Like many Central American countries, land was owned by a few wealthy families and foreign fruit companies. Honduran military has a history of controlling the country. This has helped to make Honduras one of the poorest countries in the region.

Presently Honduras has a civilian government and is now working towards giving the military less control over the country's affairs.

Honduras' economic activities consist of agriculture and manufacturing. The main exports are bananas. Up until the 1950s, Honduras was the leading producer of bananas in the world. It also exports coffee, meat and sugar. In manufacturing, food processing is the most important industry. Chemicals, clothing and cement are also produced. The country has important mineral resources such as silver, gold, and lead.

Honduras
Land: 112,088 sq km
Population: 5,000,000
Capital:Tegucigalpa (600,000 people)
Official Language: Spanish
Literacy: 59.5 per cent of adult population
Universities: 2
GNP per capita: US$560
Imports: US$957 million
Exports: US$875 million
Currency: Lempira
Government: Republic
Roads: 14,167 km

Look at a detailed map of Honduras and study its physical geography.

Write a brief summary of the people and economy of Honduras.

Nicaragua

Nicaragua is the largest nation in Central America. The central highlands reach 2,107 metres at Pico Mogotón, on the Honduran border. The Caribbean lowlands, which cover half of the territory, are drained by all major rivers and comprise the notorious Mosquito Coast. Fifty per cent of its territory is covered by forest.

The Pacific lowland area has the two largest lakes of Central America. Lake Nicaragua, the biggest, covers an area of 8,000 square kilometres. The lake's largest island, Ometepe, has two volcanoes and a population of over 28,000 people. Nicaragua has many active volcanoes. The Pacific coast is subject to severe earthquakes, and the capital, Managua, has been

The volcanoes of Concepción and Maderas on Ometepe island.

destroyed by earthquakes twice, once in 1931 and again in 1972.

About 77 per cent of the population is mestizo. Ten per cent are of European descent, 9 per cent are of African descent, and 4 per cent are indigenous people. The African and indigenous groups are found on the Caribbean coast, and speak English Creole, Garifuna and Miskito. The population is concentrated along the low, fertile Pacific coast.

The Mosquito Coast is a 65 kilometres wide littoral that borders the Caribbean Sea in eastern Nicaragua and Honduras. It is lowland of tropical forests with swamps and lagoons. The name derives from the word Miskito, the area's indigenous people. The Mosquito Coast is sparsely populated. The area had been under British control, then was later returned to the Miskitos. In 1894, it was incorporated into the Nicaraguan Republic. In 1960, the northern part was given to Honduras.

Nicaragua had been under the control of the Somoza family for more than 40 years. In 1979 the FSLN (Frente Sandinista de Liberación Nacional) took power, but from the beginning, opposition to the Sandinistas caused violence throughout the country. From a base in Honduras, the U.S. helped the right-wing contras to overthrow the Sandinista government. In 1988, a peace agreement was signed. In 1990, the FSLN agreed to call elections. Violeta Barrios de Chamorro succeeded Daniel Ortega (FSLN) as president.

✒ *Look at a detailed map of Nicaragua and study its physical geography.*

✒ *Write a brief summary of the people and economy of Nicaragua.*

The economic activity of Nicaragua consists of agriculture, mostly coffee, and manufacturing of processed foods, chemicals, metal products and textiles. The creation of the Central American Common Market (CACM) helped industries to grow in the 1950s. However, during the height of the civil war in 1978-79, fighting affected the economy and sank the country into debt. The economy of Nicaragua is still recovering from inflation and from foreign debt.

Costa Rica

Costa Rica is a mountainous country. The Cordillera Central which runs the length of the country from northwest to southeast, has several peaks more than 3,000 metres, including the Chirripo Grande (3,819 m) and the semi-active volcano Irazu (3,432 m). Wide coastal plains stretch along the east and west. The central plateau reaches an altitude of 900 to 1,200 metres and is the heart of the country. The capital of Costa Rica, San José, is located in the central mountain valley.

Costa Rica has 30 per cent of the land protected in some way, and 11 per cent is actually under natural reserves distributed in different parks throughout the country. Five per cent of the world's biodiversity is concentrated in this country. This biodiversity is seriously threatened because of the destruction of the forest.

The population is mostly of Spanish descent. The indigenous population was almost wiped out during colonial times; however, there are 35,000 indigenous people living in reserves. A

Costa Rica
Land: 50,700 sq km
Population: (1990) 3,000,000
Density: 59 persons per sq km
Capital and largest city: San Jose
(250,000 people)
Official Language: Spanish
Literacy: 93 per cent of adult
population
Universities: 4
GNP per capita: US$1,760
Imports: US$1.4 billion
Exports: US$1.1 billion
Currency: Colon
Government: Republic
Roads: 35,357 km

Rural Costa Rica.

National Theatre in San Jose, Costa Rica's capital.

Look at a map of Costa Rica and study its main physical features.

In which way is Costa Rica's past political system different to other Central American countries?

Write a short summary of the people and economy of Costa Rica.

number of people of African descent live along the Caribbean coast and came from Panama.

Costa Rica is the only Central American nation that does not have an army. Since 1889, it has had a democratic form of government. It has a good system of education and health services.

During the civil wars of the region, Costa Rica remained neutral. It supported the efforts of the Contadora Group of nations to bring peace to the region. Oscar Arias Sánchez, president from 1986 to 1990, won the Nobel Peace Prize for his attempts to end civil war through the Central American Peace Plan.

After Costa Rica became independent in 1821, the government looked for a product that the country could export. Coffee was the answer. Costa Rica was the first Central American country to grow the crop. The government offered free land to coffee growers. This enabled peasants to own land. In this way, Costa Rica avoided many of the problems due to unequal land ownership in neighbouring countries.

Today coffee is the main export, and is produced on the small farms and plantations of the country. Tourism has become the second most important economic activity. Costa Rica was the first country in the region to grow bananas and is now the second largest exporter in the world. Food crops such as corn, rice, potatoes and beans are also grown. Manufacturing is also important to the economy, and tourism has increased greatly. The Pan American Highway, which runs north to south through the middle of the country, helps greatly in moving goods.

Panama

Panama is situated at the narrowest point of the Central American isthmus, it is the only country in the world where you can swim in two oceans within the space of a couple of hours. A low mountain chain runs the length of the country. These central highlands are forested and uninhabited. The highest point in the region is Chiriqui Volcano at 3,475 m. There is a wide belt of fertile volcanic soil along the Pacific side of the central highlands.

Panama City.

Panama
Land: 77,082 sq km
Population: (1990) 2,400,000
Density: 31 persons per sq km
Capital and largest city: Panama
City (450,000 people)
Official Language: Spanish
Literacy: 90 per cent of adult
population
Universities: 3
GNP per capita: US$1,830
Imports: US$700.5 million
Exports: US$298 million
Currency: Balboa
Government: Republic
Roads: 2,745 km paved; 5,785 km
unpaved

The country has a mixture of cultures. Sixty-two per cent of its population is mestizo, 14 per cent of African descent and 10 per cent North American or European. There is also a small percentage of indigenous people. Blacks were brought from Jamaica and Barbados to help construct the Panama Canal.

Before 1903 Panama was part of Colombia. In 1903 the U.S. supported an independence movement that led to Panama's independence. Immediately after independence, Panama signed a treaty that gave the U.S. the right to construct the canal and own it in perpetuity.

The Panama Canal has served as a important means of income for the country. Although the U.S. still owns the canal, more than 80 per cent of its employees are Panamanian. It provides much of the country's employment and revenues. The economy is also based on agriculture, but industry is very small.

Panama's international banking centre is the most modern and successful in Latin America, over 100 banks from more than 32 countries operate there.

In 1968, general Omar Torrijos Herrera seized power in a military coup. He was Panama's most powerful and charismatic leader until his death in 1981. After his death, General Manuel Antonio Noriega of the Panama Defence Force gained control of the country and dissolved the government. The U.S. was concerned that the canal zone might become difficult to use. In 1989, the U.S. invaded Panama and over-threw Noriega.

Cuna indian girl from the islands off the coast of Panama.

Trace and label a map of Panama showing the Panama Canal. Mark the area controlled by the U.S.

129

The Panama Canal: a shipping shortcut

Since 1513, when Balboa first caught a glimpse of the Pacific from a mountain peak in Darién, Panama has been an important focus for trade between the Atlantic and the Pacific oceans. The history of the country has been that of a pass-route, from being the focus of violent attacks by pirates, such as Henry Morgan during the Spanish empire, to the construction in 1914 of what was seen as the greatest engineering feat of its time, the Panama Canal.

Engineers initially tried to cut a canal through Nicaragua but abandoned the idea as being too difficult. In 1882 Fernando de Lesseps, the builder of the Suez Canal, began to construct a canal through the isthmus of Panama. The vast project was abandoned in 1893 after 30 kilometres had been dug, when the company went bankrupt, the result of overspending, the difficult topography and tropical diseases which accounted for 22,000 deaths.

Work began again in 1904 in the newly independent Panama with North American investment and expertise. Work lasted for 10 years, with as many as 75,000 workers. The construction of the Panama Canal cost hundreds of lives because of the dangerous work and the mosquitoes that carried malaria. When it finally opened on 15th August 1914, the Canal cut the journey by ship south to Cape Horn by as much as 11,270 kilometres.

The Panama Canal is 50 miles long with an average width of 150 metres. The 14,000 annual canal transits take between 8 to 10 hours to pass through. Each boat is raised and lowered 85 feet from sea level to sea level by a system of three sets of locks.

Today the Panama Canal is still owned and operated by the U.S. However an agreement signed between President Jimmy Carter and Panamanian President Omar Torrijos in 1978, ceded sovereignty to the Panamanians and final transferral of ownership will take place at the end of 1999.

Chapter 17
The West Indies

The Land

The West Indian islands are the highest points of a partly submerged mountain chain. This mountain chain was formed by one of many major earth movements which have shaped the surface of the Earth.

Volcanic activity still exists on the islands of St. Vincent, Martinique and Guadeloupe. Very recently one of the volcanoes on the island of Montserrat erupted and many people were evacuated from their homes. Earth movements still occur in the West Indies, but the tremors and shocks are slight.

The West Indies is divided into two groups:

The Greater Antilles, which are the largest islands in the Caribbean, consist of Bahamas, Cuba, Hispaniola (Haiti and the Dominican Republic), Jamaica and Puerto Rico.

The Lesser Antilles consist of the major islands of Barbados, Trinidad and Tobago, Martinique, St. Kitts and Nevis, St.

✎ Trace and label a map of the West Indies. Which countries make up the Greater Antilles. Find them on your map.

✎ Which countries make up the Lesser Antilles. Find them on your map.

Most of the islands of the Eastern Caribbean are volcanic and mountainous.

Caribbean carnival.

Lucia, Grenada, Barbados and Dominica. Most of these islands were formed by volcanoes.

Most of the islands are flat except for Bahamas, Barbados, Antigua and most of Cuba, which are mountainous with the majority of land 450 metres above sea level. Coffee, cocoa and citrus grow well in the hilly areas.

The West Indies, except the northern half of the Bahamas islands, lie within the tropics of the northern hemisphere. There is very little seasonal variation in temperature.

The average annual temperature is about 28°C, or 80°F. The North-East Trade Winds bring cool winds and regulate the tropical heat. The effect of the trade winds is helped by land and sea breezes, which lower the temperatures. There are two seasons, the wet and the dry.

The British Virgin Islands.

Roseau, Dominica's capital.

Find out who were the original inhabitants of the West Indies and what was their fate.

All of these combine to give the West Indies a very pleasant climate. But there is one disadvantage: the area is vulnerable to damage by hurricanes that form in the Atlantic Ocean.

The People

The people who now make up the population of the West Indies arrived for a number of different reasons. The population is mainly of African and European ancestry. East Indian, Chinese, Middle Eastern and Garifuna are also part of the population.

The earliest occupants of the islands were the Arawaks who came from the Caribbean mainland. With the arrival of the Spaniards early in the 16th century, the Arawak people rapidly decreased in numbers. Wars and new diseases introduced by the Spaniards were the main reasons for the decline.

The Caribs also inhabited the Caribbean islands. They fought the Spaniards fiercely and prevented them from settling in the Lesser Antilles. Later on, the British, French, and Dutch conquered the Caribs and began to settle there. The Spaniards established centres of activity in Santo Domingo, Puerto Rico, Cuba and Jamaica.

The Caribbean islands were first settled because the fertile land made it possible to produce sugar cane in large amounts. However, much of the wealth produced went to the colonising countries like Britain and Spain. Sugar cane also led to the production of rum, which became a major export. Traders used rum to buy slaves in Africa after the indigenous people were exterminated. Then they returned with new slaves and traded them for the molasses used to make rum.

By the beginning of the 18th century, most of the people living in the West Indies were African slaves. When slavery was abolished in 1833, landowners had to find a different source of labour to plant and harvest their crops. People from India, China and the Middle East were brought to the West Indies as indentured labour. These events in Caribbean history explain the wide variety of peoples and cultures living in the West Indies today.

Draw a map that show European colonies in the Caribbean in the 17th century.

Which major events in Caribbean history explain the wide variety of peoples and cultures living there today?

Engraving of a 19th century sugar mill.

Jamaican beach party.

The harbour at St George's, Grenada's capital.

✐ Find out about CARICOM and share it with the class.

✐✐ What is the economy of the West Indies based on? In groups, find out about one of its main products. Discuss its production and marketing.

✐✐ What factors help to keep the islands of the West Indies closely tied to each other?

Spanish colonies fought for independence as early as the beginning of the 19th century. But the British, French and Dutch island colonies did not achieve independence until well into the 20th century. Today there are still several island colonies in the Caribbean. Most of them choose to stay that way because their small size makes it very difficult to survive without economic assistance as well as protection from international criminal activity.

Haiti became the second country in the western world (after the U.S.) to achieve independence. This makes it the world's oldest black republic. In 1844, the Spanish population on its east coast broke off into the country of the Dominican Republic.

Jamaica and Trinidad and Tobago gained their independence from Britain in August 1962. Barbados and Guyana became independent in 1966. After 40 years as a U.S. colony, Puerto Rico was granted the status of Free Associated State in 1950.

The French Islands and Guyana in South America were made departments of France in 1946. The Netherland Antilles and Surinam in South America were incorporated as autonomous states into the Kingdom of the Netherlands in 1954. After 30 years of Batista's rule in Cuba, Fidel Castro overthrew the dictator and later declared Cuba a socialist state.

The economy

Until the end of the Second World War in 1945, the economy of the West Indies was based on primary crops such as sugar. These crops were exported to Britain, France, the Netherlands and the U.S. Many foods, consumer goods and machinery had to be imported.

In the smaller islands, this dependency on imports continues. But in the larger countries such as Cuba, Puerto Rico, Jamaica, and Trinidad and Tobago, manufacturing and processing has increased. Smaller islands have also benefitted from regional trade through membership in organizations like CARICOM.

134

One of the most important new industries in the last few decades has been tourism. The smaller islands in particular have benefitted from the development of tourism facilities.

The West Indies produces many tropical fruits, spices, coffee and cacao, as well as sugar and rum. Fruit processing, textiles, mining and oil are also very important. However, many people are unemployed and a large number leave the West Indies every year to find work in the U.S.

The number of Caribbean islands spread out over a large area of sea presented problems in the past for communications. Modern technology and airports now help keep Caribbean nations abreast of changes throughout the world.

Locate the island of Cuba. Describe its main geographical features.

How is Cuba's economy different from other islands in the Caribbean?

A closer look at the West Indies

The island of Cuba is the largest island in the Caribbean. It is 1,126 kilometres long and about 40 kilometres wide at its narrowest point, broadening out to 161 kilometres in places. From the air it resembles an enormous crocodile. Because of its strategic position, it has been called the "key" to the Gulf.

Tobacco plantation in the province of Pinar del Rio.

First class hotel in Havana.

135

Cuba has three great mountain zones: the Sierra Maestra in the eastern region, Sierra del Escambray in the central region, and Sierra de Organos in the western part of the country. There, Pico del Turquino rises to 1,971 metres. Rivers in Cuba are short with very little water volume.

The flora of the islands is varied, with 800 species. Cuba's native fauna is also very rich. The smallest bird is a miniature hummingbird called *pájaro mosca*. There are no poisonous snakes in Cuba.

Jamaica was once part of the sea floor that emerged to form the island. More than half the surface is made of white limestone on top of yellow limestone. This rock contains many fossils of sea creatures.

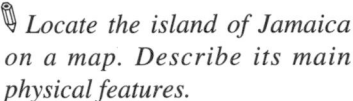 *Locate the island of Jamaica on a map. Describe its main physical features.*

The highest ground in Jamaica includes the Blue Mountains, which consist of igneous rocks. Coastal plains surround the island. Jamaica has a tropical climate. Summer temperatures are quite high, but lower slightly in the winter. Land and sea breezes moderate the heat of the day and keep the night cool. The rainfall is tropical. During the hurricane season, heavy rains sometimes bring rise to floods.

The smaller islands of the Caribbean which are called the Lesser Antilles include Anguilla, Antigua and Barbuda, Barbados, Dominica, Grenada, Guadeloupe, Martinique, Montserrat, Saint Kitts and Nevis, Saint Lucia, Saint Vincent and the Grenadines, and the Virgin Islands.

Jamaica's pepper pot soup.

Dunn's River Falls in Jamaica's northern coast.

Black sandy beach at Alligator's Pond, Jamaica.

The islands of the Lesser Antilles have varied physical characteristics, from coral limestone formed islands with bare and flat lands fringed by white sand beaches, as in the case of Anguilla, to volcanic islands with a range of high, forest-clad mountains, like Dominica and Guadeloupe. Montserrat, an island of the Lesser Antilles chain, is 17 kilometres long and 11 kilometres wide, and has seven volcanically active peaks in its mountainous terrain.

Not all islands in the West Indies are geographically located within the Greater and Lesser Antilles chains. The island of Aruba, for example, which is a part of the Kingdom of the Netherlands, lies south-west of the Lesser Antilles in the Caribbean Sea, some 80 kilometres north-west of Curacao and 29 kilometres north of the Venezuelan peninsula of Paraguana.

The Commonwealth of the Bahamas, a former British colony, lying north of Cuba, rises out of the Atlantic depths and is separated from nearby lands to the south and west by deep water channels. The Bahamas is an archipelago which comprises of nearly 700 islands, only about 30 of which are inhabited.

The Cayman Islands, a British colony in the Caribbean Sea, situated about 290 kilometres north-west of Jamaica, are the out-croppings of a submarine mountain range that extends north- eastwards from Belize to Cuba.

There are also two widely separated groups of islands about 800 kilometres apart in the Caribbean Sea called the Netherlands Antilles. The southern group of islands, of which Aruba is geographically a part, includes Curacao and Bonaire, lying about 96 kilometres off the Venezuelan coast. The northern group, including Saint Estatius, Saba, Saint Martin and Guadeloupe, geographically lies within the Leeward Islands of the Lesser Antilles.

Other islands of the Caribbean Sea which are not geographically part of the Greater and the Lesser Antilles are Trinidad and Tobago, which form the two southernmost links in the Caribbean chain of the islands; and the Turks and Caicos Islands, lying on the south-eastern periphery of the Bahamas, of which they form a physical part.

Coconut palms are common in the Caribbean.

What are the physical characteristics of the islands of the Lesser Antilles?

Make a list of nations which are a part of the Greater Antilles, the Lesser Antilles and those which do not belong to any of these groups. Name their capitals. Identify which ones are still colonies and to what country they belong.

Glossary

Alkaline - relating to substances (hydroxide) that have a bitter taste and neutralise acid. It is represented by the reaction that changes red litmus paper to blue.

Acidic - relates to substances (acids) that are sour and able to neutralise alkalis. Their effect is represented by the reaction that changes blue litmus paper to red.

Alluvial - relating to alluvium, a deposit of usually fine fertile soil left after a river or river delta has flooded its banks.

Aquaculture - the cultivation of freshwater and marine resources, both plant and animal, for human consumption or use.

Aquifer(s) - any geological formation that contains water, particularly one that supplies water for wells, springs etc.

Astronomy - science of the heavenly bodies.

Atoll(s) - a ring-shaped coral reef enclosing a lagoon.

Barrier reef - a coral reef separated from the shore by a broad deep channel.

Biodiversity - a wide variety of flora and fauna in a given area.

Biosphere - the regions of the Earth's crust and atmosphere occupied by living organisms.

Broadleaf forest - deciduous and hard-timbered trees.

Clay - the extremely fine particles of earth which are highly plastic or mouldable when wet.

Climate - weather characteristics.

Conglomerate(s) - pebbles held together by a final substance such as clay.

Cosmic gas - any air-like substance which moves freely throughout space.

Ecology - the study of the relationships between organisms and their physical surroundings.

Economy - the wealth and resources of a community, especially in terms of the production and consumption of goods and services.

Ecosystem - a system involving the interactions between a community and its non-living environment.

Environment - physical surroundings and conditions, especially as affecting people's lives.

Erosion - the wearing away of the Earth's surface by the action of water, wind, glaziers etc.

Extinct - an adjective to describe a family class or species of living creatures that has died out.

Fault - an extended break in the continuity of strata.

Galaxy - an enormous system of stars held together by magnetic attraction and separate from other similar groups, e.g. the Milky Way.

Geological - relating to geology, the science that deals with the physical history of Earth, its composition and the changes it has experienced in the past or is currently undergoing.

Indigenous - usually refering to peoples, though the term can be applied to flora and fauna that usually have existed for a long period in a given area.

Infant mortality rate - the death rate of human beings up to 12 months.

Infrastructure - the underlying framework of a system. In the case of a country it applies to transport, communication systems, hospitals etc. though these in turn have their own infrastructure.

Isthmus - a narrow piece of land connecting two larger bodies of land.

Karst - a limestone region with underground drainage characterised by caves and passages caused by erosion.

Kilometre(s) - a metric unit of measurement equal to 1,000 metres (approximately 0.62 miles).

Loam(s) - rich soil consisting of near equal proportions of sand, silt and clay particles.

Metasediment(s) - metamorphosed sediments.

Metre - metric unit of length equal to approximately 1.094 yards.

Neutral - Neither acid nor alkaline, it is the mid-point characterised by water.

Peninsula - a piece of land almost surrounded by water or projecting far into a sea or lake.

Pine Ridge - a lowland plain which is characterised by a pine savanna, low bush or grassland with palmetto clumps. This vegetation is a result of very poor soil that consist of an infertile and sandy topsoil over a very compact subsoil.

Plankton - the forms of drifting or floating organic life found in water.

Plateau - a wide, mainly level area of elevated ground.

Pollution - any discharge of material or energy into water, land, or air that destroys the Earth's ecological balance or that lowers the quality of life.

Population density - the number of inhabitants in a given area.

Rainforest - luxuriant tropical forest with heavy rainfall.

Resource - Something that a country, state etc. has and can use to its advantage.

Satellite - a man-made object put into orbit around the Earth for scientific or communications purposes.

Sediment(s) - matter that is carried by water or wind and deposited on the surface of the land that may in time become consolidated into sedimentary rock.

Soil aeration - the exchange of gases between the air and the soil.

Subsistence - a type of activity in which the produce is consumed by the producer and his family leaving, with only enough left-over to be sold or bartered for basic necessities.

Universe - the totality of all existing matter, energy and space.